Agent-based Spatial Simulation with NetLogo 2

Agent-based Spatial Simulation with NetLogo 2

Advanced Concepts

Edited by

Arnaud Banos
Christophe Lang
Nicolas Marilleau

ELSEVIER

First published 2017 in Great Britain and the United States by ISTE Press Ltd and Elsevier Ltd

ISTE Press Ltd
27-37 St George's Road
London SW19 4EU
UK

www.iste.co.uk

Elsevier Ltd
The Boulevard, Langford Lane
Kidlington, Oxford, OX5 1GB
UK

www.elsevier.com

Notices

For information on all our publications visit our website at http://store.elsevier.com/

British Library Cataloguing-in-Publication Data
A CIP record for this book is available from the British Library
Library of Congress Cataloging in Publication Data
A catalog record for this book is available from the Library of Congress
ISBN 978-1-78548-157-4

Printed and bound in the UK and US

Contents

Chapter 2. Multiscale Modeling: Application to Traffic Flow

Arnaud BANOS, Nathalie CORSON, Christophe LANG,
Nicolas MARILLEAU and Patrick TAILLANDIER

Chapter 3. Macro Models, Micro Models and Network-based Coupling

Arnaud BANOS, Nathalie CORSON, Éric DAUDÉ, Benoit GAUDOU and
Sébastien REY COYREHOURCQ

Chapter 6. Exploring Complex Models in NetLogo 173
Philippe CAILLOU, Sébastien REY COYREHOURQ,
Nicolas MARILLEAU and Arnaud BANOS

Introduction

The NetLogo platform is perfect for rapidly and effectively prototyping simple models. Volume 1, *Agent-based Spatial Simulation with NetLogo 1*, specifically focused on this remarkable quality [BAN 15a]. NetLogo also houses a number of commonly unexpected and underestimated resources that fully justify its status as a platform for agent-based modeling and simulation. These resources take two different forms. External resources allow specialized extensions to be directly constructed and/or exploited from within NetLogo, and allow NetLogo to be dynamically coupled with other libraries, software programs or platforms. The second form, more typically consisting of internal resources, arises from the suitability of NetLogo, its language and its architecture for developing models that are intrinsically more advanced. The objective of this second book is to give an educational presentation of these two important dimensions of agent-based spatial simulation with NetLogo. Readers will be offered a slightly atypical and unconventional presentation of NetLogo that emphasizes the aspect of being an open simulation environment (Chapter 1). Chapters 2–5 explore in depth the opportunities for extending and coupling NetLogo presented in the first chapter, situating them within a number of fundamental perspectives.

Chapter written by Arnaud BANOS, Christophe LANG and Nicolas MARILLEAU.

The scientific material this book relies on was developed within various research and pedagogic projects, which benefited from the financial or logistic support of several institutions: *Mission pour l'interdisciplinarité du CNRS/PEPS HUMAIN CNRS* (http://www.cnrs.fr/mi/spip.php?article193), LabeX DynamiTe (http://labex-dynamite.com/en/the-labex/), ISC-PIF (https://iscpif.fr/), RNSC (http://rnsc.csregistry.org/), MAPS Network (http://maps.hypotheses.org/).

Chapter 2 discusses the question of multiscale modeling, with applications in road traffic management, and Chapter 3 focuses on coupling macro and micro models based on networks, with applications in spatial epidemiology. Chapter 4 explores the notion of network in much more depth, considering fundamental principles of graph theory but also more advanced features like dynamic graphs. Chapter 5 focuses on solving so-called "swarm" problems. Finally, Chapter 6 brings the book to a close by presenting a number of protocols for exploring complex models in NetLogo. In the same spirit as Volume 1, this second volume includes examples of NetLogo code and GitHub links for each of the models encountered. To be read and reread without moderation!

NetLogo, an Open Simulation Environment

1.1. Introduction to extensions in NetLogo

NetLogo is a generic simulation environment in the sense that it was not designed with any specific domain of application in mind. NetLogo offers a wide range of features and generic operators to its users. Additionally, to make up for any missing features, NetLogo is compatible with other platforms and libraries, as we will demonstrate throughout this book.

There is a vast library of extensions available to users, allowing them to integrate additional functionality that is not present in the native version of NetLogo, but which might nonetheless be necessary for the development of a given model. An official library of extensions is available on the official NetLogo Website. We will explore some of these extensions later in this chapter. But many modelers have also developed their own extensions to tackle specific problems that are of interest to them. These extensions are developed with an open Java API. We will discuss this in more detail in section 1.2.

Conversely, NetLogo can also be called and controlled by other programs, such as OpenMole[1], Python[2] and R[3]. To do this, NetLogo provides a Java API

Chapter written by Benoit GAUDOU, Christophe LANG, Nicolas MARILLEAU, Guilhelm SAVIN, Sébastien REY COYREHOURCQ and Jean-Marc NICOD.

1 http://www.openmole.org/.
2 https://www.pythong.org/.
3 https://www.r-project.org/.

that allows models to be loaded, executed and gives access to their variables and methods. The usage of this API is presented in detail in section 1.3.

1.1.1. *Examples of typical NetLogo extensions*

There are many different types of extension. The GitHub page of the NetLogo platform[4] gives one possible list of examples. This list distinguishes between internally developed extensions, which are included with the platform (e.g. GIS or network), and extensions developed by the community, which have to be installed manually (section 1.1.2). In Chapter 3 of Volume 1 [BAN 15a], we presented a number of these extensions (GIS and network) to showcase some of additional functionnalities of NetLogo.

Some of these extensions include language extensions, which allow the modeler to manipulate more complex object types than those natively present in NetLogo. Indeed, the language of the platform has relatively few complex structures (unlike most programming languages) and primitives for manipulating them. For instance, the `array`, `table` and `matrix` extensions are now included with NetLogo. However, extensions such as `string` and `file` are external.

More generally, the functionalities of the NetLogo language can be augmented with a wide range of extensions, for example to achieve better network management (`network` and `nw`), to provide more primitives for network analysis (additional metrics and indicators) or to integrate geographical data represented in vector form into NetLogo models (`GIS`). This is not an easy task, but this is absolutely necessary, as NetLogo models are natively based on a grid-based discrete environment. As another example, the SQL extension allows models to interact with a database by sending SQL-formatted queries and receiving data in response. Finally, the `sound` and `MIDI` extensions allow sounds to be integrated into NetLogo models.

There are a number of extensions that enable NetLogo to interact with other tools. This interaction can take various different forms: it might simply involve reading or writing files that are compatible with a third-party application. For example, it is possible to process image files (*bitmap*), tabular data (*csv*), Java

---

4 https://github.com/Netlogo/Netlogo/wiki/Extensions.

system properties (*Props*), POV rays (*RayTracing*), VRML (*VRML*), NetCDF (*NetCDF*), etc. This allows modelers with different backgrounds to increase the realism of their simulations by exploiting real data in useful formats.

Other extensions allow deeper forms of interaction by directly integrating third-party functionality into NetLogo; for this kind of interaction, NetLogo must be able to connect with another application to send requests and retrieve results, such as Matlab (*MATLAB*), Prolog (*NetProLogo*), IODA [KUB 11] (*IODA*) and Graphstream[5] (*gs*).

For example, the NetLogo language can be extended with primitives allowing it to benefit from the scientific calculation tool R [THI 10], and in particular to call R functions from within a NetLogo model. The R extension for NetLogo can be downloaded on the Netlogo-R-Extension Website[6]. It fulfills the task of communicating data between the two tools, and in particular performs type conversions from one language to the other. A working installation of R is required. There is also a reverse extension that allows NetLogo to be called from R, known as RNetlogo[7].

Finally, there are several extensions enabling NetLogo to connect with various types of hardware (sensors, actuators, etc.). Examples include the extensions *Arduino* (microcontroller), *GoGo* (sensors) and *wiimote* (game controller with an accelerometer).

1.1.2. *Installing and using extensions in models*

The extensions used by NetLogo are located in the `extensions` folder in the NetLogo root directory. Each extension has its own separate folder.

To use an extension that is not included with NetLogo, it has to first be downloaded (usually as an archive file), unzipped and installed. Installation is extremely simple – the folder extracted from the archive has to copied into the `extensions` folder. The folder name must be the same as the name of the extension.

---

5 http://graphstream-project.org.

6 http://r-ext.sourceforge.net/.

7 http://cran.r-project.org/web/packages/RNetlogo/index.html.

To use the primitives provided by the extension in a NetLogo model, we have to first declare the extensions used by the model:

```
1 extensions [extension_name1 extension_name2]
```

To use a primitive defined in this extension, we simply call it by its name in the model prefixed by the name of the extension:

```
extension_name1:primitive_name parameters
```

For example, to extend NetLogo functionality to include additional time management functions, we can use the time extension, also known as the NetLogo Time Extension[8]. Once unzipped, the archive produces the folder time-1.3.0 (which corresponds to Version 1.3.0) containing the source files of the extension, documentation, example models and .jar files (Java archives). To use it in a NetLogo model, we have to simply rename this folder as time instead of time-1.3.0, and copy it into the extensions folder[9].

In order to use this extension, we declare it in the model:

```
extensions [time]
```

We can now use the primitives defined by this extension using the prefix time:. For example, time allows us to create a date object (with the create primitive) and to manipulate it, in order to retrieve the day, month or year of this date (get primitive), to perform operations on dates (plus primitive) or to compare dates (is-before, is-after and is-equal primitives)[10]:

---

8 https://github.com/colinsheppard/time/.

9 In fact, for this extension (and most other extensions), only the .jar files (time.jar and joda-time-2.2.jar) are required. These contain the definitions of the new primitives.

10 Other examples are included with the extension.

```
   let my_date time:create "2016-02-28 17:28:07.777"
   print time:get "month" my_date
   print time:plus my_date 1.0 "year"
4  print time:is-before (time:create "2016-01-01")
                        (time:create "2018-01-01")
```

1.2. Designing and developing extensions

A project that allows minimal extensions to be easily compiled in Scala with SBT or Maven can be found within the GitHub repository Netlogo-extension-build-example[11].

1.2.1. *Environment for compiling extensions*

1.2.1.1. *Maven and Java*

Maven is a software build management system developed by the Apache Foundation. It works by defining and using Project Object Model (POM) files, which contain a set of instructions for successfully building the program.

The first step is to install Maven on the workstation.

Maven works by relying on repositories (local or online) containing the dependencies that must be downloaded at compilation. Since March 2016, NetLogo uses the online repository Bintray[12], and it is no longer necessary to manually add the Netlogo.jar file to your local repository. Development versions (NetLogo 6.0) are already available from the online repository. However, in this book, we will use the stable Version 5.3.1.

As a reminder, since only NetLogo versions 5.3 and later are available online, we will recall how to register a .jar file in the local repository of your device. Follow the instructions given in the documentation[13]. Once you are in the NetLogo /app/ directory that you wish to install (replace X.X by the version number), you can run the following command from the command line to install the .jar file in the local Maven repository:

---

11 https://github.com/Spatial-ABM-with-Netlogo/Chapitre-A.

12 https://bintray.com/netlogo/NetLogo-JVM/netlogo.

13 https://maven.apache.org/guides/mini/guide-3rd-party-jars-local.html.

```
mvn install:install-file -Dfile=Netlogo.jar -DgroupId=org.nlogo
  ↪  -DartifactId=Netlogo -Dversion=X.X -Dpackaging=jar
```

For the development of most extensions, the Netlogo.jar file and the scala-library dependency will be enough. Other extensions that use specific NetLogo functions may, however, require other dependencies, most of which will be contained in the .jar files in the NetLogo /app/ directory.

Users who wish to develop extensions in Scala or Java will need to pay attention to the version of NetLogo. NetLogo 5.3 is only compatible with Scala versions 2.9.x, and NetLogo 5.3.1 is only compatible with Scala versions 2.10.x. In both cases, the Java version needs to be 7.x. We have to wait for the next version of NetLogo before we can use Scala 2.10.x with Java 8.x.

The simplest solution for compiling an extension is based on the modification of the JavaHOME variable used by Maven. In Linux, simply type the following command in the terminal before calling the mvn command:

```
export Java_HOME=/path/to/jdk7/
```

The pom.xml file and the Maven project that can be used to compile a minimal Java extension may be obtained from the Java-plugin-Netlogo-maven project on GitHub. This project can be directly opened in the software workbench (or IDE) Java IntelliJ.

The pom.xml file contains the list of dependencies to be loaded locally or from the Maven repositories, and also the configuration of two plugins: maven-compiler-plugin and maven-jar-plugin. The first plugin allows the Java sources to be compiled by running the Maven command mvn compile in the project root directory. The second one allows the .jar to be created in the /target repository by running the Maven command mvn install.

1.2.1.2. *SBT and Scala*

Simple Build Tool (SBT) is a build system similar to Maven, but which is commonly used to compile sources written in Scala. NetLogo is compiled with SBT, since its most recent versions are written in Scala.

Unlike Maven, which manages dependencies by using pom.xml files, SBT uses files written in Scala to determine the structure of the project and its dependencies. One of the most important such files is build.sbt, which may be found in the project root directory. SBT uses the same online repositories as Maven to download the right dependencies for compiling and packaging extensions in development. The primary SBT file, named build.sbt, uses Netlogo-Extension-Plugin[14], which automatically downloads the right Netlogo.jar file and provides a simplified interface for packaging extensions.

Since NetLogo version 5.3.1 can only be compiled with Java 7, we must tell SBT where to find this version on your device: sbt -Java-home /path/to/Java/home.

Even though it may not be immediately useful in our case, note that it is possible to tell SBT which version of Java it should use to run Java programs by adding the following lines to build.sbt:

```
fork in run := true
JavaHome in run := Some(file("/path/to/Java/home/"))
```

Finally, the extension is compiled by running the sbt compile command, and the .jar is built by calling sbt package.

1.2.2. *Notes on type conversion between NetLogo and Java/Scala*

All numeric variables used in NetLogo extensions must be converted into the Double type, as this is the only numeric type accepted by NetLogo. There are tools available to developers for converting from Java/Scala to NetLogo. But conversion in the other direction is not so easy.

Type conversion from NetLogo to Java or Scala is more tricky, in particular for LogoList lists. Since NetLogo lists are able to contain different types, it is impossible to know in advance which types of objects are contained in the list variable. The only solution is to carefully *typecast*[15] each element in the list before performing any operations.

---

14 https://github.com/Netlogo/Netlogo-Extension-Plugin.
15 Also known as type coercion, this means converting a variable from one type to another.

1.2.2.1. *Java*

From Java to NetLogo: numeric type conversion can be performed with the command `Double.valueOf(valueToConvert)`. This command wraps the `double` variables in a `Double` class, which is understood by NetLogo.

From NetLogo to Java: handling lists requires generous use of `try/catch` blocks to detect and convert the types of objects contained in the list. We will illustrate this conversion when we present the code of the primitive for calculating the average of a list of values passed as parameters.

1.2.2.2. *Scala*

Support for automatic type conversion from Scala to NetLogo has been added by the developers of NetLogo *via* the following import, which can be added to the start of a program: `import org.nlogo.api.ScalaConversions`.

Calling the function `.toLogoObject` on any Scala data type (`Boolean`, `Float`, `Character`, `Short`, `Int`, `Float`, `Long`, `Double`, `Byte`, `Seq`) initiates the conversion process, which automatically returns a type that is compatible with NetLogo.

With SBT, it is possible to initialize an *interactive console*, which can access the set of dependencies included in the project. This interactive mode allows us to enter commands directly into a terminal without having to compile or package the extension first.

In the root directory, simply type the command `sbt console` into a terminal, followed by the following commands:

```
import org.nlogo.api.ScalaConversions._

val myIntValue:Int = 5
myIntValue.toLogoObject // return Java.lang.Double
val myFloatValue:Float = 2.2
myDoubleValue.toLogoObject // return Java.lang.Double
val myScalaList = Seq(2,3,8)
myScalaList.toLogoObject // return org.nlogo.api.LogoList
```

1.2.3. *Commentary of an example extension*

The .jar file created by Maven or SBT after executing the second command includes a valid manifest file, which is usually named my-extension.jar. This should be copied into the directory /app/extensions/my-extension in NetLogo 5.3, and then called in the program with the following code: extensions [my-extension].

The extension named my-extension, which we compiled in the previous few sections, allows us to do three things:

– return the sequence of characters "hello world" (print-message);

– return the average of the numbers passed as parameters (get-mean);

– construct a list of random numbers with length equal to the variable passed as an argument to the primitive (build-a-random-list).

Calling the following command in the NetLogo observer returns the character sequence "hello world": print my-extension:print-message.

Calling the following command in the NetLogo observer returns the average of the list of numbers passed as parameters: print my-extension:get-mean list (10, 12, 15).

Calling the following command in the NetLogo observer returns a list of five random elements: print my-extension:build-a-random-list 5.

The extension code is given in Java in the below examples. Equivalent code in Scala is also available from the GitHub repository containing the examples for compilation with Maven and SBT.

1.2.4. *Minimum content of an extension*

In order for NetLogo to be capable of loading an extension, the .jar file should contain two elements: a manifest containing NetLogo-specific properties, and a class implementing the ClassManager interface of the org.nlogo.api package. The .jar file must contain all classes associated with the extension.

If additional software libraries are used, they can be placed in the extension folder in the NetLogo extensions directory.

1.2.4.1. *Manifest*

The manifest must contain the following three properties:

– Extension-Name, the name of the extension;

– Class-Manager, the extension class implementing ClassManager;

– Netlogo-Extension-API-version, the version of the NetLogo API used by the extension.

If an extension named test has ClassManager implemented by the class MyExtension in the package org.test and uses the NetLogo API 5.1, it needs to have the following Manifest:

```
Manifest-Version: 1.0
Extension-Name: test
Class-Manager: org.test.MyExtension
Netlogo-Extension-API-Version: 5.3
```

1.2.4.2. *The ClassManager*

To develop the DefaultClassManager of the extension, we can extend the DefaultClassManager class of org.nlogo.api to reduce the list of methods that we must implement for load(PrimitiveManager). Passing the PrimitiveManager object as a parameter allows us to add new primitives (commands or reporters).

Consider the following minimal example of the extension MyExtension:

```
 1  package org.test;

    import org.nlogo.api.DefaultClassManager;
    import org.nlogo.api.ExtensionException;
    import org.nlogo.api.PrimitiveManager;
 6
    public class MyExtension extends DefaultClassManager {
        @Override
        public void load(PrimitiveManager primitiveManager) throws
            ExtensionException {
          //Declare primitives
11      }
    }
```

To define the call to the three primitives, we replace the comment in the load function with the following code:

```
primitiveManager.addPrimitive("print-message", new MyMessage());
primitiveManager.addPrimitive("get-mean", new ComputeMean());
3 primitiveManager.addPrimitive("build-a-random-list", new BuildRandomList());
```

1.2.5. *Snapshot of a primitive*

The three primitives are placed in three separate Java files, each of which contains the description of a primitive:

```
2
  //BuildRandomList.Java
  public class BuildRandomList extends DefaultReporter { ... }

  //CountCharacter.Java
7 public class CountCharacter extends DefaultReporter { ... }

  //MyMessage.Java
  public class MyMessage extends DefaultReporter { ... }
```

These three classes extend the DefaultReporter interface, and so have to implement the following functions:

```
public Syntax getSyntax() {...}

public Object report(Argument args[], Context context) throws
    ExtensionException, LogoException {...}
```

In the next sections, we describe the way that these functions are called, and the results that they return.

1.2.5.1. *Displaying "hello world"*

These primitives do not take any input parameter, and simply return a message. The function Syntax.reporterSyntax() therefore only has one single argument, which indicates the expected type to be returned. Since "hello world" has the type of a string, we use the code `Syntax.StringType()`.

```
  public Syntax getSyntax() {
2       return Syntax.reporterSyntax(Syntax.StringType());
  }
```

Other types can be returned, such as `Syntax.NumberType()`, which indicates that a numerical value should be returned, `Syntax.ListType()`, indicating that a list is expected, or any other NetLogo object that can be manipulated by an extension, as shown by the list of functions defined in the `Syntax` object: `BooleanType()`, `AgentsetType()`, `TurtleType()`, `PatchType()`, `LinkType()`...

1.2.5.2. *Return the average value of an array of variable size*

We can define the call to this primitive in two different ways, either by using the syntax `Syntax.NumberType()` | `Syntax.RepeatableType()` to define a repeatable number, or by directly using a variable-size list `Syntax.ListType()`. Finally, it should also be noted that we can specify as many `Syntax.typeName` values as the number of arguments that we wish to be returned when we call the primitive. Thus, `new int[]{Syntax.NumberType()` | `Syntax.NumberType()`, `Syntax.StringType()}` indicates a primitive that takes three input arguments, i.e. two numbers and one sequence of characters.

```
  // Way 1 using NumberType and RepeatableType
2     public Syntax getSyntax() {
        return Syntax.reporterSyntax(new int[]{Syntax.NumberType() |
            Syntax.RepeatableType()},Syntax.NumberType());
    }

  // or Way 2 using ListType
7     public Syntax getSyntax() {
        return Syntax.reporterSyntax(new
            int[]{Syntax.ListType()},Syntax.NumberType());
    }
```

In the first case, the primitive is called with: print (my-extension:get-mean 0.0 5.0 10.0), and in the second case with: print my-extension:get-mean list 0.0 5.0 10.0 or print my-extension:get-mean [0.0 5.0 10.0]. The second syntax, shown below, has the advantage of being more easily understood by beginners, but requires developers to check the content of the table before performing any operations. As discussed in the previous section on type conversion, the methods for retrieving the content of the LogoList variables return a collection of Object variables that need to be tested[16].

Arguments should always be recovered using the "safe methods" provided by the developers of NetLogo, which we wrapped into a method below.

```
1  private LogoList getListOrNull(Argument args[]) throws ExtensionException,
       LogoException {
       try {
           return args[0].getList();
       } catch (LogoException e) {
           return null;
6      }
   }
```

The operation that converts LogoList logoListNumbers into ArrayList<Double> numbers is defined as follows in our code:

```
3  public Object report(Argument args[], Context context) throws
       ExtensionException, LogoException {

       final LogoList logoListNumbers = getListOrNull(args);

       // LogoList return an array of Object, so we need to cast to
           ArrayList[Double]
8      Double[] logoDouble = null;
       try {
           Object[] objectArray = logoListNumbers.toArray();
           logoDouble = Arrays.copyOf(objectArray, objectArray.length,
               Double[].class);
       }catch (ClassCastException e){
13         System.out.println("Cast Error, only numbers are supported here");
```

---

16 Both versions of the code are available from the GitHub repository online.

```
        }

        ArrayList<Double> numbers = new
            ArrayList<Double>(Arrays.asList(logoDouble));
18
        return average(numbers);

        }
```

Other conversion methods probably exist, but this topic is currently little documented on the official website. Note that in this last example wrapping the variable returned by the function average(numbers) in a Double is not strictly necessary, as Java can perform "autoboxing" in certain conditions: http://docs.oracle.com/Javase/tutorial/Java/data/autoboxing.html.

1.2.5.3. *Construct and return a table of variable size*

The first argument new int[]{Syntax.NumberType()} of the function Syntax.reporterSyntax() states that the primitive expects an integer input. The second argument Syntax.ListType() tells NetLogo that a list will be returned.

```
public Syntax getSyntax() {
    return Syntax.reporterSyntax(new
        int[]{Syntax.NumberType()},Syntax.ListType());
    }
```

Lists can be constructed using a "builder" provided by the developers:

```
LogoListBuilder list = new LogoListBuilder();
```

Adding a Double (not double) can be achieved with a simple loop as a function of the value n, assigned by calling the getIntValue() method of the class Argument on the table args[0]:

```
for (int i = 0; i < n; i++) {
        list.add(Double.valueOf(r.nextDouble()));
    }
```

1.2.6. *Future versions of the NetLogo API*

Although the NetLogo API has been relatively stable for several versions, it is expected to change with version 6.0.

Here are a couple of changes that have already been confirmed for the future version of the API:

– multiple classes will be renamed or reorganized in future. For example, a new package `org.nlogo.core` already uses classes from `org.nlogo.api`, `org.nlogo.nvm`, and `org.nlogo.agent`;

– `DefaultReporter` and `DefaultCommand` will be removed, and `org.nlogo.api.Reporter` and `org.nlogo.api.Command` will become easier to extend.

Since this version is still in development, more information can be found on the webpage dedicated to the transition[17].

Help will be available on the various channels of communication used by the developers of Netlogo: gitter[18], GitHub[19] and the NetLogo wiki, which details the extensions API[20], the discussion group[21], and the StackOverflow[22] website under the NetLogo tag.

1.2.7. *Extending the graphical interface*

The NetLogo API does not currently allow the development of dedicated graphics widgets. However, it is possible to add a new tab to the interface and directly manipulate its AWT/Swing canvas. We will use the GRAPHSTREAM[23] software library, which allows graphs to be dynamically manipulated. The purpose of the extension is to display a graph showing the set of turtles and the links between them.

---

17 https://github.com/Netlogo/Netlogo/wiki/Hexy-Extension-Transition-Guide.
18 https://gitter.im/Netlogo/.
19 https://github.com/Netlogo/Netlogo/issues.
20 https://github.com/Netlogo/Netlogo/wiki/Extensions-API.
21 https://groups.google.com/forum/#!forum/Netlogo-devel.
22 http://stackoverflow.com/questions/tagged/Netlogo.
23 http://graphstream-project.org

The following code provides the basic structure of the extension. We will later show how to develop one part of the missing content. The code is available in full on GitHub[24].

```
import org.nlogo.api.*;
import org.graphstream.graph.*;

public class GSExtension extends DefaultClassManager {
  protected Graph graph;
  protected ExtensionContext ctx;

  public Graph getGraph() { return graph; }

  public ExtensionContext getContext() { return ctx; }

  public void load(PrimitiveManager manager) throws ExtensionException {
    manager.addPrimitive("init", new DefaultCommand() {
      public void perform(Argument[] arg0, Context arg1) throws
      ↪   ExtensionException, LogoException {
        GSExtension.this.init((ExtensionContext) arg1);
      }
    });
  }

  public void init(ExtensionContext ctx) {
    this.ctx = ctx;
    this.graph = new AdjacencyListGraph("netlogo");
    this.graph.addSink(new GSNetLogoSink(this));

    addTab();
  }

  protected void addTab() { ... }
}
```

1.2.7.1. NetLogo/GraphStream connection

In a simulation, the NetLogo model and the graph coexist separately, and consistency needs to be maintained between them. Modifications affecting the NetLogo model must therefore update the graph, and *vice versa*. The GSNetLogoSink class of the extension is dedicated to managing this connection.

---

24 https://github.com/graphstream/gs-netlogo.

For the connection from NetLogo to the graph, we will use the functionality provided by the `NetLogoListener` interface of the API, which mainly consists of information about events that occur at the NetLogo interface. The method that we are interested in, `tickCounterChanged(double)`, informs us when the system undergoes a new iteration. We can therefore create events to describe the corresponding changes in the graph at these moments.

To "listen" to changes in the graph and propagate these changes to the NetLogo model, the `GSNetLogoSink` class implements the `Sink` interface of GraphStream, which connects to the graph.

`GSNetLogoSink` is structured as follows:

```
import org.nlogo.api.NetLogoAdapter;
import org.graphstream.stream.Sink;

public class GSNetLogoSink extends NetLogoAdapter implements Sink {
  protected World world;
  protected GSExtension ext;

  public GSNetLogoSink(GSExtension ext) {
    this.ext = ext;
  }

  // NetLogoListener

  public void tickCounterChanged(double arg0) { ... }

  // Sink

  public void nodeAdded(String sourceId, long timeId, String nodeId) {
  ↪   ... }

  public void nodeRemoved(String sourceId, long timeId, String nodeId) {
  ↪   ... }

  public void edgeAdded(String sourceId, long timeId, String edgeId,
  ↪   String fromId, String toId, boolean directed) { ... }

  public void edgeRemoved(String sourceId, long timeId, String edgeId) {
  ↪   ... }

  // ... other methods of Sink not used here
}
```

To establish the connection between NetLogo and GraphStream, we must create a shared procedure for identifying agents (nodes) and their connections (edges). We assume that these objects are characterized by a sequence of characters of the form breedName.agentNumber. We can therefore add a method that retrieves the identifier of a Turtle object:

```
public String getTurtleId(Turtle t) {
  return String.format("%s.%d", t.getBreed().printName(), t.id());
}
```

The tickCounterChanged(double) method needs to contain code allowing the NetLogo model to be compared with the contents of the graph. To do this, we need to iterate over the agents and their existing connections. This iteration is provided by the World object and its methods turtles() and links(). A minimal version of the function might look like this:

```
public void tickCounterChanged(double arg0) {
    Collection<Node> nodes = new HashSet<Node>();

    for (Agent a : world.turtles().agents()) {
        String nodeId = getTurtleId((Turtle) a);
        Node = ext.getGraph().getNode(nodeId);

        if (node == null)
            node = ext.getGraph().addNode(nodeId);

        nodes.add(node);
    }

    // Remove non-existent nodes
    Iterator<Node> itNodes = ext.getGraph().getNodeIterator();

    while (it.hasNext()) {
        Node n = it.next();

        if (!nodes.contains(n))
            it.remove();
    }

    Collection<Edge> edges = new HashSet<Edge>();

    for (Agent a : world.links().agents()) {
```

```
        Link l = (Link) a;
        String edgeId = getLinkId(l);
        Edge edge = ext.getGraph().getEdge(edgeId);

        if (edge == null)
            edge = ext.getGraph().addEdge(edgeId, getTurtleId(l.end1())
            ↪   getTurtleId(l.end2()), l.isDirectedLink());

        edges.add(edge);
    }

    // Remove non-existent edges
    Iterator<Edge> itEdges = ext.getGraph().getEdgeIterator();

    while (it.hasNext()) {
        Edge e = it.next();

        if (!edges.contains(e))
            it.remove();
    }
}
```

This is a minimal version of the function. It only updates the model in one direction, from NetLogo to GraphStream. Readers can refer to the project source code for more details.

1.2.7.2. *Creating a new tab*

The final part of the extension adds a new tab to the NetLogo interface on which the graph will be displayed. We will build on the addTab() method mentioned earlier. We could also add a separate primitive to make displaying the graph optional.

Tabs are managed by JTabbedPane objects (provided by Swing), which can be retrieved through the App object: App.app().tabs().

```
protected void addTab() {
    javax.swing.SwingUtilities.invokeLater(new Runnable() {
        public void run() {
            if (v != null)
                v.close();
            World w = ctx.workspace().world();
            v = new Viewer(g,
                    Viewer.ThreadingModel.GRAPH_IN_ANOTHER_THREAD);
```

```
v.setCloseFramePolicy(Viewer.CloseFramePolicy.HIDE_ONLY);
v.addDefaultView(false);

// Resize the graph to fit NetLogo.

↪   v.getDefaultView().getCamera().setGraphViewport(w.minPxcor(),
↪   w.minPycor(), w.maxPxcor(), w.maxPycor());

Tabs tabs = App.app().tabs();
tabs.addTab("GraphStream", v.getDefaultView());
    }
 });
}
```

1.2.8. *Example: the RungeKutta extension*

In this section, we will present a simple but concrete example of an extension in a few lines.

The rungekutta extension has been used for epidemiological simulation models in Chapter 3. It includes a compute-SIR function taking six Double parameters that calculates the evolution of the population stock passed as an argument using a fourth-order Runge–Kutta numerical integration method applied to the SIR equations. These equations and their solutions are described in more detail in Chapter 3.

```
override def getSyntax(): Syntax =
Syntax.reporterSyntax(Array(NumberType, NumberType, NumberType,
↪   NumberType, NumberType, NumberType, NumberType, NumberType,
↪   NumberType, NumberType, NumberType), ListType)
```

This function expects the following arguments. We will consider the case of an initial population of 100 individuals:

– the population stock S (99 susceptible individuals);

– the population stock I (1 infected individual);

– the population stock R (0 recovered individual);

– the Alpha parameter (rate of recovery I to R = 0.2);

– the Beta parameter (rate of infection S to I = 0.5/100);

– the integration step h.

The following report block passes these arguments to the function that calculates the evolution step:

```
@throws(classOf[ExtensionException])
@throws(classOf[LogoException])
override def report(args: Array[Argument], context: Context) =
{
  val S = args.apply(0).getDoubleValue
  val I = args.apply(1).getDoubleValue
  val R = args.apply(2).getDoubleValue

  val alpha = args.apply(3).getDoubleValue
  val beta = args.apply(4).getDoubleValue
  val h = args.apply(5).getDoubleValue

  rungeKuta4( Array(S,I,R), alpha, beta, h).toLogoList
}
```

Once the arguments have been safely retrieved using getDoubleValue, the values are passed to the rungeKuta4(...) function, which performs integration then returns an updated table of the SIR stock Array(ds,di,dr). We still need to convert this table into LogoList using the automatic conversion function .toLogoList.

Here is an example of how this method can be called in NetLogo:

```
show rungeKuta:compute-SIR 99.0 1.0 0.0 0.2 (0.5 / 100)
0.01
```

This call returns the following values, which describe the propagation of infection:

```
[98.99504281588354 1.0029542312962296 0.00200295282023009]
```

The source code of this extension is available in the repository for Chapter 1.

1.3. Using NetLogo from other platforms

The reason for wanting to use a NetLogo model from outside the NetLogo interface, i.e. from another language, becomes apparent as soon as we become interested in automating NetLogo simulations in batch mode (model exploration), coupling different models together (using the output of one model as the input of another), or supporting compatibility with other programs.

The NetLogo interface is useful because it allows rapid and visual development within the context of an "agile"-type approach, which means that the model is developed and then tested in fast-paced cycles, so that any change is tested as soon as it is written. The interface has graphical objects, which can be used to rapidly construct visualizations of models, and a "batch" mode, which can be used to explore models. However, there are also limitations: the graphics layout is fixed and is not necessarily suitable for operational applications. Batch mode is limited to exhaustive model exploration and only allows integrative coupling (see section 2.5). To overcome these constraints, NetLogo provides a Java API (included in the official distribution) that provides an opening to other environments. This API makes it possible to interact with the model without needing a control interface (modify simulation parameters, retrieve results, execute, etc.), as well as to modify the model (by executing NetLogo commands as if they were entered into the interface "command center"). Due to this API, we can interact with NetLogo from programs such as R or languages such as Python. As described below, this interaction unfolds according to a client/server paradigm, in which software clients such as R or Python send requests to a Java server responsible for executing the NetLogo model.

This opening to other programs allows us, for example, to:

– take advantage of all of the features of the host language (R – to exploit all of its statistical primitives, Python – to use numerical calculation libraries (NumPy[25]), Java – to use JavaFX graphics elements and any other useful libraries);

– explore NetLogo models with specific search algorithms (simulated annealing, genetic algorithms or screening), or even combinations of algorithms. Given the amount of time required to execute some simulations

---

25 http://www.numpy.org.

and the size of the parameter space, exhaustive model exploration is often impossible. Choosing a suitable exploration algorithm is the crucial first step toward obtaining results within a reasonable time frame;

– couple models by channeling the output of one model to other models with essentially zero language-related constraints due to the numerous gateways available in Java for connecting with other languages.

In the next section, we will give a brief description of the approaches that can be used to establish an interface between NetLogo and Java, Python and R. We will omit any specific details relating to the implementation, and simply explore the basic principles of a simple example of coupling.

1.3.1. *Using NetLogo from Java*

To run NetLogo commands from Java, we first need to import a library.

```
import org.nlogo.app.App;
```

In order to run NetLogo programs, the `Netlogo.jar` file needs to be located in one of the directories known to Java (`classpath`). The same is true of the `lib` directory. The latter and the `.jar` file are included within the NetLogo distribution.

We will illustrate how to use Java to run a simulation with the example of a forest fire, `Fire.nlogo`, which is included within the NetLogo distribution.

```
new Runnable() {
    public void run() {
        try {
4           App.app().open("models/Sample Models/Earth Science/" +
                "Fire.nlogo");
        }
        catch(Java.io.IOException ex) {
          ex.printStackTrace();
        }}};
```

From here, it is very simple to run NetLogo commands with *App.app.command()*, as in the below example. In this case, we assign a value to a variable and run setup.

```
  App.app.command("set number-of-turtles 100");
2 App.app.command("setup");
```

In this simulation, we need to be able to retrieve the values of the variables stored in Java. This will allow us to explore the model, either by means of sophisticated processing or suitable visual representations. To retrieve the value of a NetLogo variable, we must use the report function. In the example below, we display the value of the variable number-of-turtles.

```
  System.out.println(App.app().report("number-of-turtles"));
```

This example is based on the execution of a NetLogo model in "singleton" mode. In this mode, running multiple simulations in parallel with the same model or different models is not possible. The origin of this limitation lies in the fact that these instructions manipulate static objects. The alternative is to use the notion of "workspace". Each simulation is assigned to a workspace, and so one workspace must be created for each simulation. Each workspace acts as a wrapper for the context of the simulation with which it is associated, saving its attributes, model and execution thread.

To implement this approach, we must create an instance of the HeadlessWorkspace class with its default constructor. We can then open a model and execute NetLogo commands. The example below reuses the previous code together with the "Fire" model to execute two simulations in parallel, each with different parameters:

```
  import org.nlogo.headless.HeadlessWorkspace;
  public class SimulationFire {
      public static void startModel(int nbTurtles, HeadlessWorkspace wSpace) {
4         Runnable myThread = new Runnable() {
              public void run() {
                  try {
                      wSpace.open("models/Sample Models/Earth Science/" +
                          "Fire.nlogo");
                      wSpace.command("set number-of-turtles " + nbTurtles);
```

```
 9                      wSpace.command("setup");
                        wSpace.command("repeat 50 [ go ]") ;
                    }
                    catch(Java.io.IOException ex) {
                        ex.printStackTrace();
14                  }
                }
            };
            myThread.start();
        }
19      public static void main(String[] argv) {
            HeadlessWorkspace simulation1 = HeadlessWorkspace.newInstance();
            HeadlessWorkspace simulation2 = HeadlessWorkspace.newInstance();
            SimulationFire.startModel(100, simulation1) ;
            SimulationFire.startModel(200, simulation2) ;
24      }
    }
```

More details on these features are available on the NetLogo GitHub page[26]. There are technical subtleties relating to memory consumption, controlling threads and the choice of whether to execute *via* a graphical user interface (GUI) or the command line (Headless).

As well as allowing multiple executions, each with its own context, the Java API provides the key to interoperability with other platforms and development languages. Java has many possibilities and gateways to other languages (C, Python, R, etc.). The NetLogo APIs developed by the community for other programming languages build on these gateways and the native Java API distributed with NetLogo. In the next part of this section, we will consider two examples showing how to use NetLogo from other languages and applications: Python and RNetlogo.

1.3.2. *Using NetLogo from Python*

Python is a programming language widely used in science, and its popularity continues to grow. It has many different libraries, in particular *NumPy*, which is extremely useful for scientific computations and numerical simulations of mathematical models based on differential equations.

With *NumPy*, Python can be viewed as a way of combining mathematical models and multiagent models. Python also proves very useful for dynamically generating experimental protocols and automatically executing them.

---

26 https://github.com/Netlogo/Netlogo/wiki/Controlling-API.

There is no direct interface between Python and NetLogo. This means that a Java bridge (JavaGateway) is required, running as a background task. This bridge receives the NetLogo commands from Python and executes them in the model to obtain the desired results.

One example of such a Java bridge was developed by David Masad, and is available on the webpage *Bad Networking*[27]. We will distribute a modified version that allows multiple simulations to be executed. The sources and executable of the modified version can be downloaded from the GitHub page of this book, at https://github.com/Spatial-ABM-with-Netlogo.

The idea is to run a Java program that will act as a server. The Python program uses a library (package) that allows it to connect to this server. Each time that Python wishes to access NetLogo, it sends a request to the Java program. This program then executes the instructions in the NetLogo model to obtain the desired results.

Thus, executing a NetLogo model form Python unfolds in the following stages:

1) check that the Java bridge is running in the background, otherwise start it up;

2) connect Python to the Java-NetLogo bridge;

3) create as many workspaces as required to run simulations;

4) initialize the simulations with the right parameters;

5) execute the simulations;

6) analyze the results.

The Java server program works according to the above steps. An example of Java and Python code allowing multiple simulations to be simultaneously executed from Python and Java commands is available on the GitHub page of this book.

---

27 http://davidmasad.com/blog/Netlogo-from-python/http://davidmasad.com/blog/Netlogo-from-python/.

Once you have checked that the `Java-Netlogo` bridge is running properly, you need to create a `JavaGateway` object to establish a connection with the Java server.

```
# import
from py4j.Java_gateway import JavaGateway

# connect Python to the Java-Netlogo bridge
5 gw = JavaGateway()
bridge = gw.entry_point
```

It is now relatively simple to open an example model by creating a workspace in Java, which is identified by a number in Python:

```
# create one workspace for each simulation we wish to run
sample_models = "/Applications/Netlogo 5.0.2/models/Sample Models/"
forest_fire = "Earth Science/Fire.nlogo"
4 wks1 = bridge.createWorkspace()
wks2 = bridge.createWorkspace()
bridge.openModel(wks1,sample_models + forest_fire)
bridge.openModel(wks2,sample_models + forest_fire)
```

We can now execute the NetLogo commands by specifying the desired workspace with its number (this procedure is specific to our interface):

```
# Initialize the simulations with the desired parameters
# Parameters of the 1st simulation
3 bridge.command(wks1,"set density 62")
bridge.command(wks1,"random-seed 0")
bridge.command(wks1,"setup")

# Parameters of the 2nd simulation
8 bridge.command(wks2,"set density 50")
bridge.command(wks2,"random-seed 2")
bridge.command(wks2,"setup")

# Run the simulations
13 bridge.command(wks2,"repeat 50 [go]")
bridge.command(wks1,"repeat 50 [go]")

# Process the results of the simulation
...
```

We can now retrieve the values of the variables and display them:

```
    ...
  2 # Process the results of the simulation
    burned_trees = [0]*2
    burned_trees[0] = bridge.report(wks1,"burned-trees")
    burned_trees[1] = bridge.report(wks2,"burned-trees")

  7 print "the average number of burned tree is: ",
        sum(burned_trees)/float(len(burned_trees))
```

As you can see, this works the same way as Java, except that we can now use the advanced features offered by Python to automatically execute a parametrized series of models and construct all sorts of visual results, for example using libraries such as matplotlib.

1.3.3. *Exploring and analyzing models with R*

NetLogo can be called from R using RNetlogo[28]. As presented in the article (https://www.jstatsoft.org/article/view/v058i02), this package is also based on the NetLogo Controller API (in Java), with an additional layer that provides a connection between Java and R. The package can be installed as usual with the following command in R:

```
install.packages("RNetlogo")
```

Once the package is installed, it simply needs to be loaded. This must be performed once for each NetLogo session, and is done with the following function:

```
library("RNetlogo")
```

---

28 http://rNetlogo.r-forge.r-project.org/.

We can now run NetLogo from R. As was the case for Java, there are two available modes: GUI and headless, i.e. with a graphical interface or from the command line. To launch the GUI mode[29]:

```
install.packages(c("JGR","Deducer","DeducerExtras"))
```

To actually run it, we need to execute the following commands:

```
  Sys.setenv(NOAWT=1)
  library(JGR)
  Sys.unsetenv("NOAWT")
4 JGR()
```

Next, run NetLogo:

```
1 nl.path <- "/Applications/Netlogo 5.3.1/Java/"
  NLStart(nl.path)
```

We can now control NetLogo with R. For example, we can load a model (or in our example a library of models using the function NLLoadModel in R), execute commands on models (with the function NLCommand) and modify the values of model parameters or execute individual model methods (for example, setup then go).

```
  ;; Load a model
  model.path <- file.path("models", "Sample Models", "Earth Science",
      "Fire.nlogo")
3 model.library.path <- "/Applications/Netlogo 5.3.1/"

  NLLoadModel(file.path(model.library.path, model.path))
  ;; Execute commands on this model
  NLCommand("set density 77")
```

29 The path is the path to the folder with the Netlogo.jar archive. However, users running Mac OS X or Linux who wish to run NetLogo in GUI mode will need to use JGC. The installation steps are given on this page: http://www.deducer.org/pmwiki/pmwiki.php?n= Main.MacOSXInstallation.

```
8  NLCommand("setup")
   NLCommand("go")
   NLDoCommand(10, "go")
   NLDoCommandWhile("ticks < 200", "go")
```

We also need to be able to retrieve the values of variables. This can be done very simply with the NLreport() command.

```
burned <- NLReport("number-of-turtles")
```

As you can see, running NetLogo from R is relatively simple. This allows you to exploit the powerful calculation functions available in R to explore your models.

1.3.4. *Discussion*

The three examples given above show that accessing and externally controlling a NetLogo model passes through the Java interface distributed with each version of NetLogo.

Java is an expressive language, which makes it possible to develop links to most platforms and languages. The communities of the most commonly used languages in science, such as R and Python, have already created implementations of these links (RNetlogo and Python-Netlogo respectively). Most of these links seem to follow a common pattern, using primitives to load the NetLogo model and then execute commands written in NetLogo.

If the need should ever arise, the Java interface could definitely be used to develop an *ad-hoc* links with specific functionality. This is the principle behind the Open-Mole platform, a distributed environment for model exploration, which we will discuss in section 5.6.

1.4. Deploying NetLogo models online

As well as the classical NetLogo application installed on personal computers, which comes with a well-stocked library of models, NetLogo also exists on the Internet. The NetLogo Web[30] application is similar to the desktop version (with somewhat reduced functionality) and can be accessed from a web browser (section 1.4.1). The NetLogo community is extremely active on the Internet and on a number of Websites for publishing models. In the next section, we will present the two best-known of these websites: Modeling Commons[31] dedicated to distributing NetLogo models (section 1.4.2) and the more general-purpose web portal OpenABM[32] for publishing and sharing models (section 1.4.3).

1.4.1. *Netlogo Web*

NetLogo Web (http://www.Netlogoweb.org) is one of the official Internet websites of the NetLogo platform. It gives not only a download link for the desktop application, but also provides access to an online implementation of NetLogo *via* the web browser (see the section presenting NetLogo 1.1).

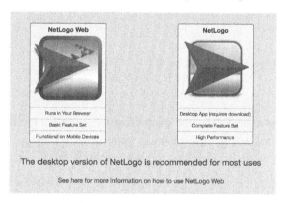

Figure 1.1. *NetLogo Web homepage (March 2016)*

The web version of the NetLogo application allows you to run the models available on the platform, but you can also upload your own models. The usual features are available: the command center, the code editor and information relating to the model description. You can run the application as if it were

---

30 http://www.Netlogoweb.org/.
31 http://modelingcommons.org/account/login.
32 https://www.openabm.org/.

installed on your personal computer. There are, however, some restrictions, as some features are not yet available. For example, extensions, some language-specific primitives, file reading and writing, 3D models and `BehaviorSpace` are not yet available.

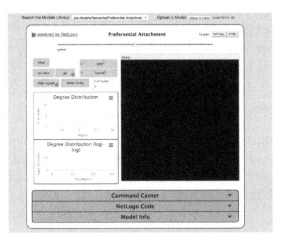

Figure 1.2. *Interface of one of the models available online (March 2016)*

Therefore, if your model uses one of the features unavailable in the online version, you will need to use the desktop version of NetLogo. If not, this platform is a great way of running models without having to install the application (Figure 1.2).

1.4.2. *Modeling Commons*

Modeling Commons[33] (Figure 1.3) is an Internet-based platform for facilitating collaboration between NetLogo modelers. Users can share their models, as well as edit, create and execute them.

The platform also allows users to save their own personal models, and specify the level of visibility. Models can be set to private, or restricted to a certain specific group of users.

---

33 http://modelingcommons.org.

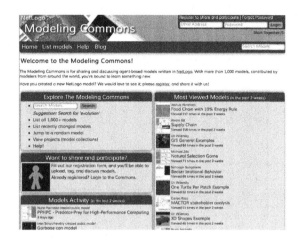

Figure 1.3. *Modeling Commons homepage (March 2016)*

The first step is to create a user account (using the platform is completely free). This is only required if you wish to save models online, edit them, or comment on existing models. Browsing and downloading public models do not require logging in.

You can now upload a model (Figure 1.4). The platform will ask you to specify the name of the model, provide the filepath on your computer and optionally upload an image as an illustration. The reading and writing permissions of the model must then be selected. The model can be set to either public or private – collaborators can always be added at a later point.

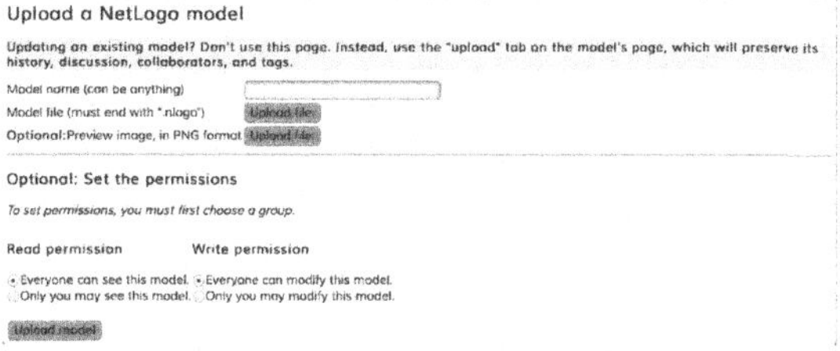

Figure 1.4. *Interface for uploading a model (March 2016)*

Permissions can be changed by adding collaborators. You can also write a model description and browse other related tabs: comments, model execution, code, version history, auxiliary model files, models belonging to the same family (we will return to this concept later) and an update tab (Figure 1.5). This final tab allows you to upload an updated version of the model.

Figure 1.5. *Model management window (March 2016)*

The History tab gives an overview of all versions, and allows you to download each of them. You can also revert to a previous version.

Finally, the update function allows you to create a child version of the current parent model. Child models are created by performing the classical operation of forking, as is common practice within the programming community. The development of the parent and child models then follows independent paths. However, the relationship between the two remains visible in the History tab.

In summary, the Modeling Commons platform is oriented toward sharing NetLogo models. It provides simple and easy-to-access functionality. The ability to manage groups and organized models into projects helps to develop an effective workflow.

1.4.3. *OpenABM*

OpenABM is a consortium that unites teachers, researchers and professionals with the objective of promoting agent-based modeling. The Website[34] (Figure 1.6) offers a large collection of resources on related topics.

---

34 http://www.openabm.org.

They already have a very extensive library of community-submitted models. Each model is documented, and the source code is provided.

Figure 1.6. *OpenAbm.org homepage (March 2016)*

But this platform is much more than just a repository of agent models. The *Education* section of the website contains an extensive range of tutorials and documentation for helping to develop models. There are also links to online courses, textbooks and a YouTube channel[35].

A comprehensive selection of resources is available, such as links to development platforms, the websites of modeling-related journals and a well-stocked reading list. There is also a calender of topical events, a forum and job opportunities.

More than anything else, OpenABM is a platform for sharing models and resources on agent-based modeling. As a tool, it is truly comprehensive.

1.5. Conclusion

In this chapter, we showed how the openness of the NetLogo platform holds the key to a great amount of potential.

This is reflected first and foremost in its extensions, which are numerous. We non-exhaustively listed a couple of examples that we consider to be particularly significant, such as *array, R, gis, sound, raytracing*, etc.

---

35 http://www.youtube.com/user/CoMSESNet/.

We also took the opportunity to explain how to install and use NetLogo extensions, and showed how to personally design a new extension. We gave a list of compilation environments and explained the mandatory content of a minimal extension.

In section 1.3, we examined the possibility of using NetLogo from other platforms. We considered the cases of Java, Python and R. There are other platforms that can make calls to NetLogo, such as OpenMole, an environment dedicated to exploring models using high-performance computations. We will discuss this further in section 5.6.

Finally, we discussed the different ways of deploying models on the Internet. NetLogo Web allows models to be executed online, and Modeling Commons provides additional features to support collaboration. We ended the chapter by presenting OpenABM, a privileged hub for resources on relevant topics.

2

Multiscale Modeling: Application to Traffic Flow

2.1. Introduction

Traffic modeling is a particularly active field, the origins of which can be traced back to the pioneering work of Greenshield in the 1930s [GRE 35]. Greenshield was the first to formulate a structural relation between the speed of vehicles on a road and the distance between them. This relation between the flow rate/density, at the heart of the so-called fundamental diagram (see Figure 2.1), has been used by all families of traffic flow models developed ever since. These families of models can be grouped into three distinct but strongly interconnected subcategories: macroscopic models, which consider flows of vehicles, microscopic models, which consider individual vehicles and their interactions, and mesoscopic models, which lie in between the other two categories.

Each of these families of models, and hence each of the models themselves, have a number of specific properties. The aim of this chapter is to introduce some of these models, and show how they can be dynamically linked together.

Chapter written by Arnaud BANOS, Nathalie CORSON, Christophe LANG, Nicolas MARILLEAU and Patrick TAILLANDIER.

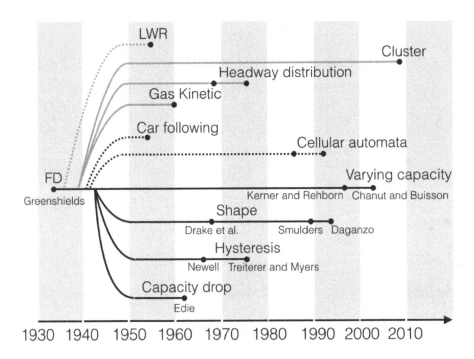

Figure 2.1. *Genealogy of traffic flow models based on the fundamental diagram, reproduced from[1] [WAG 15]. The top branch represents the foundations of macroscopic models. The origins of mesoscopic models are shown in grey, and those of microscopic models in dashed line. The lower branches correspond to theoretical developments relating to the fundamental diagram. For a color version of the figure, see www.iste.co.uk/banos/netlogo2.zip*

2.1.1. *Coupling models together*

Each model is only applicable and valid in certain restricted circumstances. For instance, a traffic flow model developed for a section of highway will not be directly applicable to intraurban situations, which have a completely different road network morphology and driving regimes.

Linking models together is a natural way to expand their scopes of application. Model coupling provides conceptual methods and tools

---

1 The full diagram, which is much more comprehensive and also shows the connections between different models, can be accessed online at doi:10.1007/s13676-014-0045-5.

specifically designed to combine models with each other to produce new models that can be applied to questions and contexts outside of the scope of each of the initial models.

The question of which models to couple obviously depends on the goals of the final model, but crucially also depends on the validity and relevance of each model with respect to the research question.

2.1.1.1. Weak, strong and integrative coupling

There is no single correct way to formulate or represent coupling. But at the very least, there must exist links between models: these are called coupling factors. The connections between models can be:

– *Direct*: the models describe different dynamics (epidemic and mobility), but these dynamics are nevertheless based on a shared description of system components (for example, the same individuals are modeled by both models). One or more of the links might then be obvious, resulting in natural coupling.

– *Indirect*: the models describe different dynamics (epidemic and mobility), and each model has its own separate representation of the system components (e.g. individuals/populations). The link between these models is no longer natural, and transformation functions are required.

There are three main approaches for implementing the actual coupling:

– *Integrative coupling*: this is the most common approach. The principle is to transform and combine the models in order to construct a larger model. Substantial design, development and validation phases are crucial for perfecting these kinds of models, which require prior methodological planning on how the models will be coupled and combined.

– *Weak coupling*: this is the simplest approach. The models are executed according to some workflow. The models simply exchange inputs/outputs (the output from one model is the input of the other), and so remain independent. One of the limitations of this approach relates to dynamics with competitive, temporal or spatial aspects, as these factors cannot be taken into account without implementing scaling procedures.

– *Strong coupling*: this approach instead considers competitive, temporal and spatial aspects as the determining factors of the model dynamics. Submodels are executed in parallel and share information throughout the simulation. Model synchronization techniques are needed to ensure that the models are anchored to meaningful "space-times".

Integrative and strong couplings introduce a high level of interdependency between the coupled models. This must be controlled with algorithmic tricks and tried-and-tested techniques to ensure that the models remain consistent.

2.1.1.2. *Ensuring temporal consistency*

When designing a model, the time scale is a crucial choice that must be made early in the modeling process, as it affects all subsequent choices. Changing the time scale of a model involves reconsidering the relevance and representations of all modeled dynamics, and will often require the model to be rebuilt. In strong and weak couplings, it is therefore important to conserve the time scale of each constituent model. If this is not possible, an integrative approach should be used.

This raises the question of how to combine models with different time scales without having to modify them. To do this, we need to identify a global time scale that encompasses the time scales of each model.

One typical approach is to distinguish continuous models (e.g. mathematical models based on ordinary differential equations or partial differential equations) from discrete models (such as Markov chains, cellular automata or multiagent systems).

Continuous models are easy to link together, as the language of mathematics provides a number of tools for ensuring consistency between models. Discrete models on the other hand are more difficult to connect. In these models, time is divided into atomic time units that can take three forms:

– *Fixed time steps*: atomic time intervals that represent a physical duration separating two moments at which the model is evaluated. This duration is chosen arbitrarily after considering the model dynamics. This is the approach most commonly employed by agent-based models.

– *Variable time steps*: atomic time intervals that represent a variable physical duration. This duration is determined by the model as a function of the intensity of its dynamics (the more a given dynamic affects the phenomenon being studied, the shorter the time step). Numerical simulation methods such as Runge–Kutta are based on this principle, and coupling tools such as *"Virtual Soil"* also use it.

– *Events*: timestamped actions that trigger the next evaluation and update the model. These actions are located on a timeline of events. The simulation aims to unravel this timeline. Coupling approaches such as DEVS [ZEI 97] and HLA [AWA 13] are based on this method.

To couple models together, it is crucial to choose a common unit of time so that their execution can be synchronized. Choosing the time scale of a model is similar to determining the sampling frequency of a signal. Smaller time scales improve the precision, but increase the cost (computing time and model complexity), and can lead to modeling inconsistencies (by calculating a value to an excessive degree of precision relative to the precision of the available data). However, if the scale is too large, the dynamics of the system may not be visible. Choosing a suitable time scale is critical, as it strongly influences subsequent results.

The most common method for selecting this scale is to determine the largest time step that divides each of the time steps of the coupled models (the GCD of the time steps – greatest common divisor). This approach is the simplest to implement, but can be expensive, as all models are evaluated at the smallest time scale, resulting in excessively many evaluations.

The second approach is to use a variable time step. A default time step is selected based on the dynamics of the system. Shortly before executing a model, the time step is subdivided into smaller time steps to match the time scale of this model. Once the model has finished its execution, the time step returns to its default periodicity.

However, the method that seems to be widely preferred by coupling platforms is to consider the time step as a periodic event just like any other event in a discrete-event model. It then becomes natural to link models with different time scales: the time steps and events are gathered and combined along a single execution thread that symbolically represents continuous time. The execution of the coupled model therefore translates into the successive execution of an ordered list of timestamped events, which gradually advances the simulation time.

2.1.1.3. *Ensuring data consistency*

Consistency of the data is ensured by techniques and tools that implement formalisms such as DEVS [ZEI 97] and coupling platforms, either general-purpose such as FMS [VAL 12], HLA [AWA 13] and VLE [QUE 05], or specialized such as Records [BER 10] and Virtual Soil. These coupling environments characterize models as a black box equipped with input and output parameters. Models are connected together with transition functions responsible for scaling the outputs of one model to serve as the inputs of the next, while ensuring that the data remain consistent with respect to time.

This view of coupling shows the interest in having simple descriptions for the links between the models: the resulting model is similar to a workflow scheduled by a discrete-event clock.

These approaches quickly reach their limits when attempting to model spatial phenomena. Each model has its own representation of space, which may be private. This makes it difficult to describe competition for spatial resources, which is essential in certain areas, such as soil sciences. This seems to be ultimately due to the mathematical and non-spatial origins of these formalisms.

More recently, a new perspective has taken the opposite approach to historical methods by making space the central component around which the coupling is constructed. Space is represented as a special zone in which interactions between models result in competition and stigmergy. Within this framework, space itself must be modeled at multiple scales by using special architecture, such as holonic [HAS 12] or pseudo-fractal [BLA 09] structures, to provide the spatial connection between models operating at different scales.

This approach is highly relevant in the domain of urban dynamics, and can be used to model the socioeconomic phenomena of urban growth. Cities are often viewed as multiscale spaces hosting different kinds of processes (demographic growth, economic growth, public sector growth, etc.) each of which carries a spatial footprint (living quarters, venues for economic and universal services). It then becomes natural to situate these processes within a virtual, multiscale space representing a city. These processes can then interact and cohabit in space, as is readily observed within urban systems.

2.1.1.4. *Traffic*

Traffic flow simulation illustrates both the added value and the difficulty of model coupling. Traffic can be understood at different scales according to whether we consider vehicles individually (microscopic scale and discrete approach) or vehicle flows (macroscopic scale and continuous approach). Most models are formulated at a single scale, which limits the set of questions in their fields of applications to which they can provide answers. Model coupling can be used to overcome these limitations, in particular by coupling macroscopic and microscopic models. However, a number of questions must be resolved in order to implement this coupling, as we saw in the previous section.

To illustrate some of the possible answers to these questions, we propose a very simply case study of automobile traffic on a closed circuit with *NumEdges* edges, each of which is characterized by:

– a fixed length;

– a speed limit;

– a fixed critical concentration;

– one single lane (overtaking is not possible).

The critical concentration parameter is important at macroscopic scales, since vehicles are considered as a flow rather than strictly individually. Three distinct but closely interdependent values must be taken into consideration:

– the average speed of the vehicles on the road (V);

– the concentration of vehicles on the road (K), which is given by the number of vehicles on the road divided by the length of the road;

– the flow rate (Q), which corresponds to the number of vehicles that pass through a certain point over a given time interval.

These quantities usually satisfy the relation $Q = K.V$, which lies at the heart of traffic theory and forms the basis of the so-called fundamental diagram [GRE 35].

The vehicle flow (macro scale) or the individual vehicles (micro scale) travel along the circuit, passing from one edge to the next, indefinitely. In the microscopic case, the transitions between edges are modeled as follows: when each vehicle arrives within a distance of less than ϵ from its destination node, it is immediately moved onto the node, and is assigned a new destination. For consistency, the value of this parameter is chosen to be less than the distance that a car can travel at the speed limit on this edge.

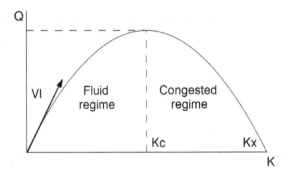

Figure 2.2. *Fundamental traffic diagram ([BOU 03]), showing the flow Q as a function of the concentration K*

Figure 2.3. *The road is a closed circuit composed of one-way edges of single-lane traffic. At initialization, the vehicles all start on the same edge*

There are many models for describing traffic. In this chapter, we will explore three of them throughout the next few sections: the macroscopic LWR model, the mesoscopic Underwood model and the microscopic NaSch model. Each model corresponds to a specific scale of traffic, and is based on either an agent-based formalism (abbreviated to ABM for agent-based model) or an equation-based formalism (EBM for equation-based model). These terms are listed in Table 2.1.

Figure 2.4. *If a vehicle is at a distance of less than ϵ away from its destination node, it is moved directly onto the node*

Model	View of traffic	Formalism
LWR	Macro	EBM
Underwood	Meso	ABM
NaSch	Micro	ABM

Table 2.1. *Scales and formalisms of the considered models*

2.2. Two agent-based models: NaSch and Underwood

In these two models (NaSch and Underwood), vehicles are represented individually. The difference between the two models lies primarily in the way that vehicles adjust their speeds. On each edge, vehicles adjust their speeds according to different processes, depending on whether we choose the NaSch model or the Underwood model (the latter of which exists in multiple variants).

2.2.1. *The NaSch model*

The NaSch model, named after its creators, Nagel and Schreckenberg, initially started as a cellular automaton model (see [NAG 92, SCH 02, SCH 95]), but can be converted to an individual-based model (see [GOD 07, BAN 09]).

In this model, each vehicle i located on edge j is characterized by:

– its speed, $Speed_i$, satisfying $0 \leq Speed_i \leq MaxSpeed_j$, where $MaxSpeed_j$ is the speed limit of edge j;

– the Euclidean distance from the vehicle k that precedes it, D_{ik}.

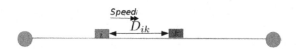

Figure 2.5. *The NaSch model takes into account the speed $Speed_i$ of the vehicle i (which is less than the speed limit), and the distance from the vehicle in front (D_{ik})*

```
to compute-Dn
    let Dist-Nxt-Nde distance-next-node
    if any? cars with [my-current-edge = [my-current-edge] of myself and
        distance-next-node < Dist-Nxt-Nde]
4   [
        let Distmax max [distance-next-node] of cars with [my-current-edge =
            [my-current-edge] of myself and distance-next-node < Dist-Nxt-Nde]
        set Dn Dist-Nxt-Nde - Distmax
    ]
end
```

Initialization: the initial speed of the vehicles is chosen to be the speed limit of the edge minus a random amount between 0 and 20% to introduce heterogeneity into the initial speeds of the vehicles.

```
to initialize-NasCh-speed
2 ask cars
    [
        set speed [max-speed-patch-tick] of my-current-edge - random-float 0.2 *
            [max-speed-patch-tick] of my-current-edge
    ]
    end
```

The parameters $NaSchFactor$ and $NaSchNoise$ are defined between 0 and 1, and are involved in updating the speed (acceleration or deceleration) of each vehicle. The NaSch model follows the rules stated below at each time step t.

Acceleration: assuming that drivers wish to travel as quickly as possible, if the vehicle is not currently at the speed limit, its speed is increased by $NaSchFactor$:

$$Speed_i = \min(Speed_i \times (1 + NaSchFactor), MaxSpeed_j)$$

```
  to accelerate
    let MinComp1 min ( list ( [max-speed-patch-tick] of my-current-edge ) (
        speed + speed * NaSch-Factor) )
    set speed max ( list 0 MinComp1 )
4 end
```

Deceleration: assuming that drivers wish to avoid collisions, and that speed is equivalent to a certain distance traveled per time step, if the distance from the vehicle in front is less than or equal to $Speed_i$, the speed is decreased by setting its value to:

$$Speed_i = min(Speed_i, D_{ik} \times (1 - NaSchFactor))$$

```
1 to decelerate
    let MinComp2 min ( list ( speed ) ( Dn - Dn * NaSch-Factor ) )
    set speed max ( list 0 MinComp2 )
  end
```

Random variability: assuming that drivers can overreact, or that their speed can fluctuate close to the speed limit, the speed of each vehicle is randomly decreased by $Speed_i \times NaSchFactor$ (while always remaining positive) with a certain probability. Hence, if (random-float1) $< NaSchNoise$:

$$Speed_i = max(Speed_i - Speed \times NaSchFactor, 0)$$

```
1 to randomization
    if speed > 0
    [
      if ( random-float 1 ) < NaSch-Noise
      [
6       set speed max (list 0 ( speed - speed * NaSch-Factor ))
      ]
    ]
  end
```

Movement: the distance traveled in each time step t by each vehicle on an edge is equivalent to the value of $Speed_i$. Each vehicle moves once per time step as a function of its speed.

```
 1  to adapt-speed
      let Dist-Nxt-Nde distance-next-node ; my distance from the next node
      if speed < [max-speed-patch-tick] of my-current-edge and Dn > speed
      [
        accelerate
 6    ]
      if ( any? cars with [my-current-edge = [my-current-edge] of myself and
          distance-next-node < Dist-Nxt-Nde] ) and ( Dn <= speed )
      [
        decelerate
      ]
11  end

    to NaSch-model
      update-distance-next-node
      ask cars
16    [
        compute-Dn
        adapt-speed
        randomization
      ]
21  end
```

2.2.2. *The Underwood model*

The Underwood model [UND 61] operates at mesoscopic scales. The speed of each vehicle is updated as a function of the number of vehicles on each edge, independent of their relative positions (see Figure 2.6). We are therefore interested in the concentration of vehicles on the edge, and not their positions. In this model, the speed of the vehicles is taken to be equal to their free speed, i.e. the speed limit on the road: $Speed_i = MaxSpeed$, weighted by the concentration of vehicles on the edge. The Underwood function depends on the concentration ($CurrentConcentration$) and the capacity ($Capacity$) of the edge:

$$Speed_i = MaxSpeed * exp(\frac{-CurrentConcentration}{Capacity})$$

```
to update-car-speed-underwood
  ask cars
  [
4       set speed ( [max-speed-patch-tick] of my-current-edge ) * exp(- ((
            [current-concentration] of my-current-edge ) /
            ([num-max-cars-on-edges] of my-current-edge) ))
  ]
  end
```

Figure 2.6. *The Underwood model allows all vehicles to travel at the speed limit when the edge is empty, and then reduces their speed exponentially as the concentration on the edge increases*

NOTE.– In its simplest version, this model has three fundamental limitations. First, it is unsuitable for situations with high concentrations, as the speed of the vehicles is reduced to zero if the concentration on the edge strongly exceeds its capacity. Furthermore, it is largely deterministic. The only potential source of randomness is from the scheduling of agents in an asynchronous implementation such as the one chosen here. Finally, it does not consider the relative positions of vehicles, and can result in illogical situations. For example, a vehicle is slowed down by the presence of other vehicles behind it.

We therefore propose two variations. The first, referred to as *"Underwood-Random"*, simply introduces a random component into the model. The second, which we will call *"Underwood-Forward"*, considers the relative position of vehicles on each edge, while retaining the mesoscopic character of the reference model.

Underwood-Random model: introducing a random component into the model can be done very simply when the speed is calculated by penalizing each vehicle by a random factor proportional to its speed (random-float $\times (speed \times Underwood - Factor)$):

```
    to update-car-speed-underwood-random
      ask cars
      [
4         let speed-underwood ( [max-speed-patch-tick] of my-current-edge ) *
             exp(- (( [current-concentration] of my-current-edge ) /
             ([num-max-cars-on-edges] of my-current-edge) ))
          set speed max (list ( speed-underwood - random-float (speed *
             Underwood-Factor)) 0)

      ]
      end
```

Underwood-Forward model: for each vehicle, when calculating the speed, only the concentration of vehicles on the part of the edge in front of the vehicle is considered.

Thus, the speed of a vehicle is determined by the Underwood-Random function, which depends on the concentration and the capacity not of the whole edge, but only the part located in front of the vehicle (see Figure 2.7):

```
    to update-car-speed-underwood-forward
2     update-distance-next-node
      ask cars
      [
        let Dist-Nxt-Nde distance-next-node
        let my-edge my-current-edge
7       let forward-concentration count cars with
        [(my-current-edge = my-edge) and (distance-next-node < Dist-Nxt-Nde)]
        let speed-underwood ( [max-speed-patch-tick] of my-edge ) * exp (-
           (forward-concentration / (([num-max-cars-on-edges] of my-edge) *
           (Dist-Nxt-Nde / [edge-size-patch] of my-edge))))
        set speed max (list ( speed-underwood - random-float (speed *
           Underwood-Factor)) 0)
      ]
12  end
```

This refinement of the initial model produces a considerable change in the traffic dynamics. We observe an increase in the average speed (of around 10 km/h on average in the example), a stabilization in the speed of the fastest vehicles, which are no longer affected by the vehicles behind them, and an equally significant decrease in the concentration (see Figure 2.8).

Figure 2.7. *The Underwood-Forward model allows all vehicles to travel at the speed limit when they are alone, but forces them to reduce their speed as a function of the number of vehicles present in front of them on the edge, as well as the capacity of this part of the edge*

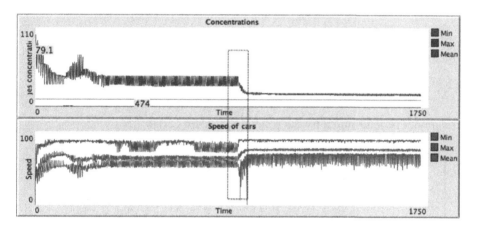

Figure 2.8. *Impact of the "Forward" component in an Underwood model with 10 nodes. The rectangle shows the point at which Underwood-Random was replaced by Underwood-Forward*

2.3. An equation-based LWR model

The LWR model [LIG 55, RIC 56] is a flow model inspired by fluid mechanics that was proposed by Lighthill, Whitham and Richards in 1955. Whereas the models presented above consider vehicles individually, this model represents traffic as a continuous flow (macroscopic scale). It is based on collective behaviors and builds on the fundamental diagram (see Figure 2.9), which shows the equilibrium states of traffic and hints at the relationship between concentration and flow rate. This kind of model can be used to describe phenomena relating to movements and congestion.

The LWR model makes the following assumptions:

1) The road is divided into sections of length x.

2) Time is divided into steps of duration t.

3) The concentration is uniform on each section.

4) A vehicle cannot travel across more than one section in a single time step.

In this section, we will use the following notation (see [BOU 03]):

– $Q(x, t)$ = flow rate: number of vehicles that pass through x at time t;

– $K(x, t)$ = concentration: number of vehicles present at time t on a section x of the road;

– $V(t, x)$ = average speed of the vehicles located at x at time t.

The model is determined by the following system [2.1]:

$$\begin{cases} Q(x,t) = K(x,t) \times V(x,t) \\ \dfrac{\partial Q(x,t)}{\partial x} + \dfrac{\partial K(x,t)}{\partial t} = 0 \\ V(x,t) = V_l\left(K(x,t)\right) \end{cases} \qquad [2.1]$$

The first equation is the fundamental rule: $Q = K \times V$.

The second equation is the rule of conservation of traffic. The variation over time in the concentration depends on the inflow and outflow of vehicles. This corresponds to the change in the flow rate over space.

The third equation is the fundamental diagram of traffic, presented for the first time in [GRE 35] (see Figure 2.9). This equation allows us to write the speed as a function of the concentration. So long as the concentration remains below the critical concentration of the road, vehicles can travel at the speed limit (or free speed V_l). But if the critical concentration is attained, the speed decreases and a congestion phenomenon occurs.

Note that in the case of the LWR model, the critical concentration must be equal to half of the maximum concentration.

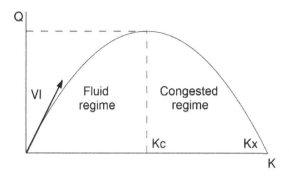

Figure 2.9. *Fundamental diagram of traffic [BOU 03]*

Numerical integration of the LWR model: The LWR is a system of partial differential equations (PDEs). In order to numerically integrate it, we use the following space-time discretization method presented by Godunov (see [LEB 96]). We need the following notation: Δx is the discretization step for dividing the road into sections (Δx is the length of section i). Since Δx is constant, all sections are the same size.

Δt is the discretization step in time.

The flow rate is assumed to be constant during each time step, which justifies dividing up space to ensure that the speed does not remain constant over too large a distance. Accordingly, we assume that it takes Δt to travel over the length of the space step Δx.

Calculating the inflow and outflow for each section: For each section, we define the supply and demand functions as follows: the *supply* is the number of vehicles able to enter a section, and the demand is the number of vehicles wanting to leave a section.

Let:

– Qx = maximum flow rate;

– Kc = maximum concentration;

– Vl = maximum speed (free speed).

Lebacque showed that the flow rate can be calculated by introducing the supply functions (S) and demand functions (D) as shown in Figure 2.10.

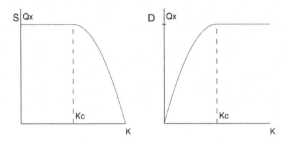

Figure 2.10. *Supply (S) and demand (D) functions according to concentration (K), defined in [BOU 03]*

We chose to represent these supply and demand functions in a simplified/linear form as shown in Figure 2.11.

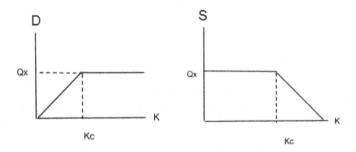

Figure 2.11. *Simplified representation of the supply and demand functions*

The demand function can also be written as the function [2.2]:

$$D(K(x,t)) = \begin{cases} \dfrac{Q_x}{K_c} K(x,t) & \text{if } K(x,t) \leq K_c \\ Q_x & \text{if } K(x,t) \geq K_c \end{cases}$$

[2.2]

This function can be implemented with the following code:

```
   to OfferFunction
     ifelse current-concentration <= critical-concentration
 3   [
       set offer max-flow
     ]
     [
       set offer max list 0 ( (- max-flow / critical-concentration) *
           current-concentration + 2 * max-flow )
 8   ]
   end
```

The supply function can in turn be written as the function [2.3]:

$$
O(K_i) = \begin{cases} Q_x & \text{if } K(x,t) \le K_c \\ \dfrac{-Q_x}{K_c} K(\dot{x},t) + 2Q_x & \text{if } K(x,t) \ge K_c \end{cases}
\qquad [2.3]
$$

This gives the following code:

```
 1 to DemandFunction
     ifelse current-concentration <= critical-concentration
     [
       set demand max list 0 ( ( max-flow / critical-concentration) *
           current-concentration )
     ]
 6   [
       set demand max-flow ;
     ]
   end
```

Let $K_i^{t+\Delta t}$ and $Q_i^{t+\Delta t}$ be the concentration and the flow rate in section i at time $t + \Delta t$:

$$
Q_i^{t+\Delta t} = \min \left(D(K_i), O(K_{i+1}) \right)
$$

$$
K_i^{t+\Delta t} = K_i^t + \frac{\Delta t}{\Delta x} \left(Q_{i-1}^{t+\Delta t} - Q_i^{t+\Delta t} \right)
$$

$$\qquad [2.4]$$

The first equation of [2.4] states that, for a given section i, the flow rate at time $t+\Delta t$ is equal to the minimum of the vehicles that wish to exit i and those that can enter the next section. In other words, if fewer cars wish to exit the section i than can enter the next section, everyone will be able to get through. This gives the following code:

```
1 to UpdateFlow
    ask nodes with [any? my-out-edges]
    [
      set nxt-offer [offer] of one-of my-out-edges
    ]
6   ask edges
    [
      set current-flow min list demand [nxt-offer] of end2
    ]
  end
```

The second equation of [2.4] states that the concentration of section i at time $t + \Delta t$ is equal to the concentration at time t plus the number of vehicles exiting the previous section $(i - 1)$ minus the number of vehicles exiting the section i. This gives the following code:

```
  to UpdateConcentration
    ask nodes with [any? my-in-edges]
    [
      set prvs-flow [current-flow] of one-of my-in-edges
5   ]
    ask edges
    [
      set previous-flow [prvs-flow] of end1
      set current-concentration ( current-concentration + ( 1 /
        max-speed-patch-tick ) * ( previous-flow - current-flow ) )
10  ]
  end
```

One of the assumptions behind these equations is that a vehicle cannot travel further than the next section within a single time step, which can be mathematically written as: $\dfrac{\Delta x}{\Delta t} \geq V_l$ where V_l is the maximum speed.

This simple model cannot reproduce phenomena such as the accordion effect in traffic jams, clustering or phases of acceleration/deceleration. Finally, the LWR model represents uniform traffic moving from one equilibrium state to another, but does not give a correct description of transition phases. This is why we are interested in a hybrid model that will allow us to couple the LWR model with other models that operate at microscopic scales.

2.4. Hybrid traffic model

The hybrid or coupled model developed here refers to a model in which the representation of traffic is equation-based on some parts of the road and agent-based on others (see, for example, [BOU 03, ABO 14, BUR 06]). Figure 2.12 shows a diagram of this kind of hybrid model.

Passing from one representation to another like this presents several challenges. We need to go from a real number of cars (continuous representation) to an integer number of cars (discrete representation). We also need to take into account the fact that the spatial and temporal dimensions are not represented in the same way in both models.

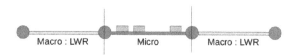

Figure 2.12. *Representation of a hybrid traffic model*

We will continue to consider the example of a closed circuit divided into $NumEdges$ edges. The traffic on each edge is modeled either by an equation-based LWR model, or by an agent-based NaSch or Underwood model.

Vehicles: The transition LWR $\rightarrow$ NaSch/Underwood requires us to derive an integer number of vehicles from a continuous flow. To implement this transition from a real number (flow) to an integer (vehicles), we will take the integer part of the real number to create vehicles, and save the decimal part, which will accumulate until it reaches a unit, at which point a new vehicle is created. This accumulation-based system ensures that the number of vehicles is conserved.

For the transition agent $\rightarrow$ LWR, vehicles need to be added to the flow and removed as individual vehicles. Therefore, we will add them to the concentration on the LWR section, and delete them from the list of agents.

```
   to generateCars-From-LWR [nb]
     ask end2
     [
 4     let considered-edge one-of my-out-edges
       if [LWR-Section] of considered-edge = 0
         [
           hatch-cars nb
           [
 9           set my-current-edge considered-edge
             set current-node [end1] of my-current-edge
             set next-node [end2] of my-current-edge
             ask my-current-edge
             [
14             set current-concentration current-concentration + 1
             ]
             set concentration-of-my-current-edge count cars with
                 [my-current-edge = [my-current-edge] of myself]
             set size 0.4
             set shape "arn-car-yellow"
19           update-my-position
           ]
         ]
     ]
   end
```

Space and time: To ensure that time (and consequently speed) is handled consistently, we chose to subdivide the LWR sections into subsections. In the case of LWR, one subsection is traversed per time step, whereas the speed of vehicles is managed according to the specific logic of the NaSch or Underwood approaches defined as above for individual-based models.

To determine the number of subsections in each LWR section, and ensure that time is handled consistently, we assume that a vehicle traveling at the speed limit on a NaSch or Underwood section requires time T to travel across this section. If there is no congestion (i.e. at free speed), we know that only one single time step is required to travel across an LWR subsection. Therefore, subdividing an LWR section into T subsections will ensure that, at free speed, traveling across an LWR section is equivalent to traveling across an NaSch/Underwood section.

The number of subsections in each section therefore depends on their length and speed limit, as shown in Figure 2.13.

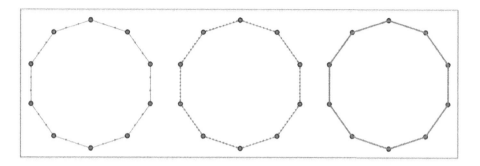

Figure 2.13. *The edges are divided into subedges of equal size. With a fixed speed limit, the number varies as a function of the length of the road (here, respectively* 1, 3 *and* 6km*)*

We begin by determining the number of intermediate nodes per edge in terms of the length of the edge and its free speed:

```
set num-subedges int ( [edge-size-patch] of one-of edges /
    [max-speed-patch-tick] of one-of edges )
```

We then create nodes for each edge, positioning them equidistantly:

```
to generate-SubNodes
  if traffic-function = "LWR" and not any? edges with [lwr-section = 1]
4 [
    ask edges
    [
      set lwr-section 1
    ]
9 ]
  ask edges with [lwr-section = 1]
  [
    let edge-length edge-size-patch
    let i 0
14  repeat num-subedges - 1
    [
      set i i + 1
      ask end1
      [
19      let ref who
        hatch-nodes 1
```

```
      [
        set reference-node ref
        set sub-node 1
24      set i-node i
        set size size / 2
        set shape "dot"
        set color white
        fd (edge-length / num-subedges) * i
29      ]
        set nb-subnodes i
      ]
    ]
  ]
34 end
```

Finally, subedges are created in such a way that each intermediate node is connected with the node before and the node after. These intermediate nodes might overlap with the initial nodes of the graph if placed at the beginning or the end of an edge:

```
1 to generate-SubEdges
    ask edges with [lwr-section = 1]
    [
    ask end1
    [
6    let me who
     let my-Subnode one-of nodes with [reference-node = me and i-node = 1
         and sub-node = 1]
     create-edge-to my-subnode
       [
         set sub-edge 1
11       set lwr-section 1
         set shape "link-arn2"
         set color green
         set thickness 0.05
       ]
16   ]
    ]
    if num-subedges > 2
    [
    ask nodes with [sub-node = 1]
21   [
       let next-Subnode one-of nodes with [reference-node = [reference-node]
           of myself and i-node = ([i-node ] of myself + 1) and sub-node = 1]
       if is-agent? next-Subnode
       [
       create-edge-to next-subnode
26       [
           set sub-edge 1
```

```
              set lwr-section 1
              set shape "link-arn2"
              set color green
31            set thickness 0.05
            ]
          ]
        ]
      ]
36   ask nodes with [count out-link-neighbors = 0 and sub-node = 1 ]
       [
         let my-next-node one-of other nodes with [sub-node = 0 and who !=
             [reference-node] of myself] with-min [distance myself]
         create-edge-to my-next-node
         [
41           set sub-edge 1
             set lwr-section 1
             set shape "link-arn2"
             set color green
             set thickness 0.05
46         ]
       ]
     end
```

The interface of the hybrid model is shown in Figure 2.14. There are three LWR sections. The vehicles are colored yellow on "Underwood-Car-Forward" sections. They merge into the flow in the LWR sections, and reappear at the end of these sections. The red nodes show that the flow is not necessarily uniformly distributed over each LWR section, but can vary over its subsections depending on when and how the vehicles arrive.

2.5. Conclusion and outlook

This chapter develops a simple example to introduce readers to traffic modeling, and shows how to compare and dynamically couple models that operate at very different scales. In particular, we coupled a macroscopic model (LWR) with a mesoscopic model (Underwood and its variants) and a microscopic model (NaSch). While implementing this coupling, we made sure to observe the fundamental constraint of conserving the number of vehicles, but we also ensured that the flow speeds remained consistent in each of the coupled models.

The proposed implementation in NetLogo is fairly generic, and can easily be extended to support more complex models, either by developing its structural components (in particular the choice of road network) or by elaborating on the processes themselves. In its current state, this model can be used in experiments to more systematically compare the behavior and performance of each of the models presented above, and in particular to explore the performance of the hybrid model as the size of the road network and the number of vehicles increases. This is a crucial step in adaptively utilizing the possibilities of each model.

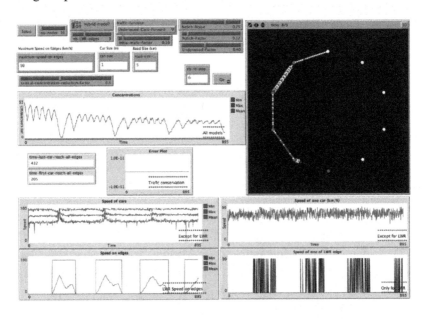

Figure 2.14. *Interface of the full model, coupling LWR sections and Underwood-Forward sections. For a color version of the figure, see www.iste.co.uk/banos/netlogo2.zip*

Macro Models, Micro Models and Network-based Coupling

3.1. Introduction

In this chapter, we will discuss coupling models with different scales to describe the propagation of a virus within a population. This population is distributed throughout a set of cities connected by airline routes. Population movements between cities enable the virus to travel, carried by infected individuals. In each city, the description of virus propagation is based on an SIR-type model (presented in more detail in section 3.2). The first model, called EpiSim [DAU 14], is presented in section 3.3, first in its aggregate variant, and then in its individual-based variant. Comparing these two approaches will allow us to discuss the advantages and limitations of each of them. In the second section, we will present two approaches for coupling models based on networks. The first approach considers a network of coupled systems of equations (section 3.5). The second combines an agent-based model of microscale components with a model of macroscale components based on systems of equations (section 3.6). This coupled model, called MicMac, is presented in more detail in [BAN 16]. The added value of micro/macro coupling is examined in the article [BAN 15b].

This chapter picks up where the last chapter left off. In the previous chapter, we considered a weak coupling approach combining distinct traffic models

Chapter written by Arnaud BANOS, Nathalie CORSON, Éric DAUDÉ, Benoit GAUDOU and Sébastien REY COYREHOURCQ.

with different scales. This chapter instead focuses on an integrative coupling approach that associates two different dynamics modeled at different scales.

3.2. Description of the equation-based SIR model

The dynamics of an epidemic within a population can be formulated with an SIR model that describes the evolution of the number of susceptible (S), infected (I) and recovered (R) individuals within the population. This model is described by the system [3.1] (see [KER 27]).

$$
\begin{cases}
\dfrac{dS}{dt} = -\dfrac{\beta}{N}IS \\[2mm]
\dfrac{dI}{dt} = \dfrac{\beta}{N}IS - \alpha I \\[2mm]
\dfrac{dR}{dt} = \alpha I
\end{cases}
\tag{3.1}
$$

In this model, each city has a population (P) divided into three groups S, I and R. If the population has not been previously exposed to the virus, then P = S, and everybody in the city is susceptible. The population is constant, i.e. demography is not taken into account. The transition from the group of susceptible individuals to the group of infected individuals is described by the term $\dfrac{\beta}{N}SI$ where $\dfrac{\beta}{N}$ is the contamination rate in the event of contact between a susceptible individual and an infected individual. The transition from the group of infected individuals to the group of immune (recovered) individuals is described by αI, where the α term gives the proportion of infected individuals that recover at each time step.

This system of equations describes the evolution of the number of susceptible, infected and recovered individuals over time for fixed contamination and recovery rates, as shown in Figure 3.1.

There are various different approximation methods for numerically calculating the solutions of this kind of system, i.e. determining the evolution of S, I and R over time. As discussed previously (Volume 1, Chapter 5, p. 178 [BAN 15a]), the system dynamics module in NetLogo uses Euler's method. We will use this module and hence this method for section 3.3 of this chapter. In section 3.3, the numerical method that we will use is called fourth-order

Runge–Kutta ([BAN 15a] p. 183). It is implemented directly in NetLogo. Finally, in section 3.6, we will use the Scala extension presented in Chapter 1 of this book.

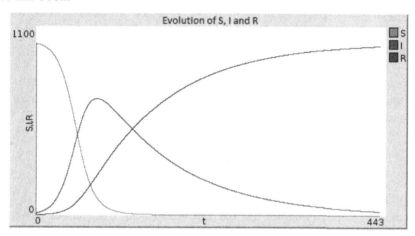

Figure 3.1. *Evolution of the number of susceptible, infected and recovered individuals over time with $\alpha = 0.2$, $\dfrac{\beta}{N} = 0.5$ (hence, R_0 is equal to $\dfrac{\beta}{\alpha} = 2.5$) and initial conditions $S_{init} = 1000$, $I_{init} = 10$ and $R_{init} = 1$. The chosen method of numerical integration is Runge–Kutta 4, with a resolution of 10^{-3}. For a color version of the figure, see www.iste.co.uk/banos/netlogo2.zip*

In the following sections, whenever an SIR system is used to describe the population of a city i (for $i \in 1, ..., NBNodes$), we will denote the S, I and R components of the populations respectively, by S_i, I_i and R_i.

3.3. Equation-based and agent-based propagation model: EpiSim

In this section, we will aim to recreate the global dynamics of the aggregate SIR model with an agent-based model. We will analyze the conditions under which each of these two models converge and diverge. We will begin by individualizing the SIR model without spatial constraints, and then we will gradually add mechanisms for local interactions.

3.3.1. *Distributed and non-spatial SIR model*

The first stage of modeling is to develop the processes of the aggregated mathematical model using an agent-based formalism

(EpiSim_Modele.nlogo), while retaining the fundamental assumptions of the initial approach (EpiSim_Math_Modele.nlogo). To shift from the first formalism to the second, we need to redistribute the SIR model at the individual scale. Each agent is therefore assigned a description of its epidemiological state: $S \rightarrow I \rightarrow R$. Similarly to the aggregate version, these transitions are not symmetric.

In this first stage, space is not considered, and each agent can potentially interact with everyone, depending on the contact rate β. The graph of interactions is said to be trivial. Each agent has two transition functions:

$$P(S \rightarrow I) = \beta \frac{I}{N} \quad \text{and} \quad P(I \rightarrow R) = \alpha$$

This non-spatial model, shown in Figure 3.2, is agent-based, but still reproduces the same dynamics as the equation-based SIR model given equivalent initial conditions.

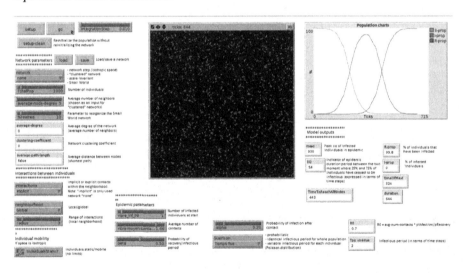

Figure 3.2. *Screenshot of the dynamics of the non-spatial model. The* Network *parameter is set to "None", the* interactions *are "implicit" (each agent can potentially interact will every other agent), the* neighborhood *is "global" and individual mobility* (IndividualStatic?) *is currently irrelevant*

3.3.2. *Spatially distributed SIR model with local interactions*

In this second version of the model, the individual probabilities of transition are calculated as a function of a local fixed-radius neighborhood of agents (fixed Euclidean distance around the agent). At each time step, the agents have unlimited mobility within the domain. In this spatial version of the model, individuals are randomly distributed over space at initialization and at each time step. Contacts occur randomly within the neighborhood of each agent, which can be configured to be more global or local depending on the choice of spatial constraints. Thus, no *a priori* structure is defined for potential contacts. The graph of contacts that did actually occur during the simulation could, however, be reconstructed *a posteriori*, to examine its topology.

$$P(S \rightarrow I) = \beta \frac{I_{local}}{N_{local}} \quad \text{and} \quad P(I \rightarrow R) = \alpha$$

Under these conditions, the model shown in Figure 3.3 once again allows us to obtain dynamics similar to those produced by the equation-based SIR model.

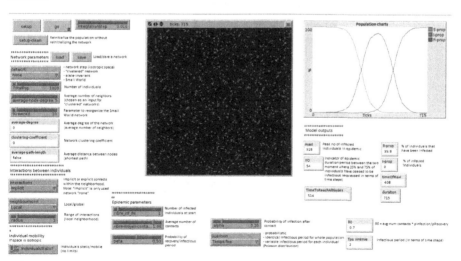

Figure 3.3. *Screenshot of the dynamics of the spatial model with local neighborhoods. The* Network *parameter is still set to "None",* interactions *remain "implicit", the* neighborhood *is now "local" with a fixed* radius *of 3 and individual mobility* IndividualStatic? *is disabled*

3.3.3. *Spatially distributed model with local neighborhoods and explicit contact between individuals*

We continue this approach with a fully distributed and behavioral model, shown in Figure 3.4. Each agent S experiences a number n of contacts (parameter `avg-num-contact`), which follows a Poisson distribution with mean β. Each agent therefore effectively enters into contact with n agents from its neighborhood V. If the state of one of these n neighbors is I, then $S \rightarrow I$.

$$P(S \rightarrow I) = 1 \quad \text{if} \quad \sum_V I \geq 1 \quad \text{and} \quad P(I \rightarrow R) = \alpha$$

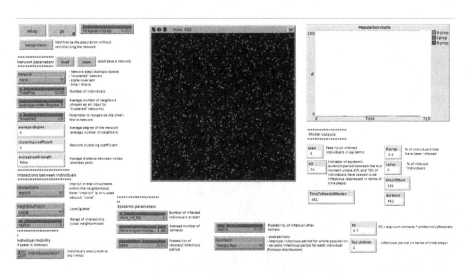

Figure 3.4. *Screenshot of the dynamics of the spatial model with local neighborhoods and interactions only between individuals. The* Network *parameter is still set to "None",* interactions *are now "explicit", the* neighborhood *remains "Local" with a fixed* radius *radius of 3 and individual mobility (*IndividualStatic?*) is either enabled or disabled*

The dynamics produced by the simulations of this model deviate from previous dynamics, and infection rates are lower than previous versions, or completely absent. One way of verifying this is to vary the radius, IndividualsStatic? mobility and avg-num-contact parameters to trigger the dynamics of an epidemic. These results allow us to improve the model by relaxing the hypotheses of global spatiality and global interaction. The next model therefore takes into account the movements of agents and the localized nature of the contacts that could potentially result in virus transmission.

3.3.4. *Spatially distributed SIR model with a network of interactions*

With this next version, the structure of potential contacts can be entered as a model input to specify the network of interactions between agents. Each agent is represented by a node, and its potential contacts are represented by a set of connections making up its neighborhood. Hence, mobility is no longer relevant here, since the network of interactions does not change over the course of the simulation. At each time step, each agent comes into contact with other agents selected from the set of level 1 neighbors within the network, limited to the average number of contacts retained from the previous version of the model (fixed parameter β which follows a Poisson distribution). In other words, if the size of the neighborhood is less than `avg-num-contact`, then this parameter takes the value of the size of the neighborhood. Other networks can be constructed in order to study the role of topology in the dynamics of virus propagation:

– Regular networks: networks such that all vertices have the same number k of neighbors, also described as k-regular networks.

– Random networks with fixed degree distributions: networks whose vertices have an average of k neighbors. This number varies locally around the mean for each vertex. The number of edges is defined beforehand to guarantee the desired degree distribution, then each edge is connected to two randomly selected vertices.

– Small world networks: intermediate networks between regular networks and random networks. To generate these networks, we start with a regular network and randomly reassign a certain percentage of its edges.

– Scale-free networks (scale-invariant): directed acyclic or star networks with a strongly heterogeneous distribution for the number k of neighbors of each node. This distribution follows a power law.

These networks can be characterized by global topological indicators such as:

– the average degree K: the average number of incident edges to a vertex;

– the clustering coefficient C: this measures the degree to which the network contains clusters, i.e. groups of vertices strongly linked together and weakly connected to the rest of the network;

– the average of the $C(x)$ evaluated at each vertex x: this is the number of existing edges within the neighborhood $K(x)$ of the vertex x divided by the number of possible edges in this neighborhood;

– the average length of shortest paths: the average of the shortest values for the distance between any two vertices of the network.

We will present the results of simulations performed with a clustered network, such that k-degree equal to 6 (Figures 3.5 and 3.6) and 2 test parameter values corresponding to the high/low values for L. For example, when the network has a high k-degree, the clustering coefficient C is high, and the average of the shortest distances L tends to be low. By contrast, the lower the k-degree of the network, the higher the average of the shortest distances tends to be.

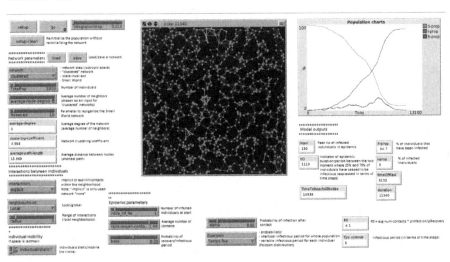

Figure 3.5. *Screenshot of the dynamics of the spatial model, network with interindividual interactions. The value of* avg-num-contact *remains fixed at 1.66. The* Network *parameter is set to "clustered", with* average-node-degree *equal to 6. The* α *(0.50) and* β *(0.20) parameters have been adjusted to obtain a higher* $R0$ *(4.1)*

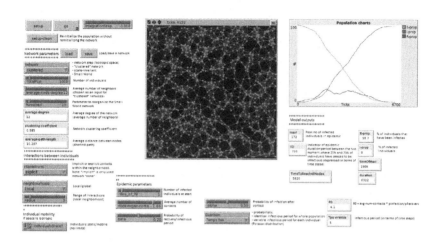

Figure 3.6. *Screenshot of the dynamics of the spatial model, network with interindividual interactions. The value of* `avg-num-contact` *remains fixed at 1.66. The* `Network` *parameter is set to "clustered", with* `average-node-degree` *equal to 12. The* α *and* β *parameters have been adjusted to obtain a higher* $R0$ *(4.1)*

The simulation calculates several indicators as outputs: the proportion, of the entire population, of the contaminated individuals at peak contamination (`MaxI`); the interquartile range (`IQR`), which provides an indication of the duration of the epidemic; and the cumulative percentage of infected individuals once the epidemic is over (`Recovered`). In general, the simulations confirm the initial intuition that the more the network is connected, the faster the virus propagates through it, and the greater the number of infected nodes.

Studying the influence of the $R0$ parameter on these indicators and varying the k-degree parameter shows the "compensating" effect of this parameter relative to how the degree of network connectivity affects the propagation dynamics. Recall that the $R0$ parameter is equal to the probability of infection multiplied by the average number of contacts divided by the probability of recovery. The simulations show a strong time shift as a function of the k-degree parameter: the epidemic "takes off" more quickly as the network connectivity increases, for fixed $R0$. This can be observed by comparing the two experiments shown in Figure 3.5 (11340 ticks) and Figure 3.6 (6322 ticks). A simple experiment (varying $R0$, varying the k-degree parameter) allows this initial intuition to be quickly verified. Also, the $R0$ threshold value for a "lightning" epidemic (hyper-fast epidemic that reaches all vertices within a short period) decreases as the connectivity increases. Note also that the value of $R0$ required for the epidemic to affect almost all of the population may be less than 1 if the network is strongly connected.

3.4. Coupling SIR models based on networks

Assume now that we have the same nodes as the previous models, representing cities, but that the edges between these cities represent connections by air. We also define a mobility rate g for each city, representing the proportion of outbound travelers from that city. This proportion may vary across the groups of susceptible, infected and recovered individuals. We could, for example, assume that in the case of a symptomatic disease, infected individuals will cease to travel, whereas asymptomatic individuals will continue to do so. With this assumption, the number of infected individuals is a function of the proportion of asymptomatic cases observed for a given infectious disease. The mobility rates are, respectively, denoted by gi, gs and gr. The mobile population of city i is therefore given by $g(S_i + I_i + R_i)$, or by $(gsS_i + giI_i + grR_i)$ in the case where the mobility varies as a function of infectious state.

Once these mobility rates have been defined, individuals from one city can travel to adjacent cities. The weight m_{ij} of each edge is the fraction of outbound travelers from node i headed toward node j. The sum of the m_{ij} corresponding to each of the outbound edges at a given node must be equal to 1:

$$\sum_{j=1,\, j\neq i}^{N} m_{ji} = 1 \text{ with } m_{ii} = 0$$

Thus, these nodes and edges define a network of cities, and the population moves through them. To model these movements, we propose two approaches.

3.5. SIR coupling without scaling: Metapop model

3.5.1. Presentation of the Metapop model

The metapopulation approach considered here takes into account the flow of travelers from one city to another at each time step of the simulation. Trips are assumed to be instantaneous (the Euclidean distance between any two cities is zero) since the model does not naturally include a notion of time and its dynamics are exclusively defined by the number of integration steps. We are therefore only interested in the epidemic-related dynamics of the city network, as shown by the model in Figure 3.2.

$$
\begin{cases}
\dfrac{dS_i}{dt} = -\dfrac{\beta}{N}I_iS_i - gs_iS_i + \displaystyle\sum_{j=1}^{n} gs_j m_{ji}S_j \\[2mm]
\dfrac{dI_i}{dt} = \dfrac{\beta}{N}I_iS_i - \alpha I_i - gi_iI_i + \displaystyle\sum_{j=1}^{n} gi_j m_{ji}I_j \\[2mm]
\dfrac{dR_i}{dt} = \alpha I_i - gr_iR_i + \displaystyle\sum_{j=1}^{n} gr_j m_{ji}R_j
\end{cases}
\qquad [3.2]
$$

Note that at each node, these dynamics are given by the initial dynamics of the epidemic after subtracting all outbound travelers (hence the term $-gs_iS_i$ in the group of susceptible individuals) and adding all inbound travelers from adjacent cities j (hence the term $\displaystyle\sum_{j=1}^{n} gs_j m_{ji}S_j$ in the susceptible group). Movements are instantaneous, and at each step of the simulation the total population is given by the sum of the populations at each node.

The interface of the metapopulation model is presented in Figure 3.7.

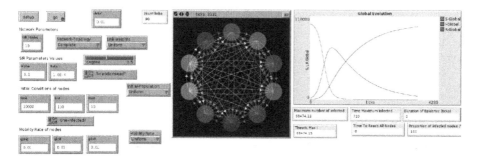

Figure 3.7. *Interface of the metapopulation model, allowing the user to define the network topology as well as the mobility rates and the initial distribution of the population. This allows us to observe not only the dynamics of single nodes, but also those unfolding at the level of the whole network. For a color version of the figure, see www.iste.co.uk/banos/netlogo2.zip*

3.5.2. Numerical integration of a network of coupled SIR using Runge-Kutta implemented in NetLogo

The fourth-order Runge-Kutta method is used to numerically approximate the solutions of systems of ODEs. Recall that it works by averaging four estimates, which makes it more precise than other approaches such as the Euler method. Its implementation in NetLogo is shown below for an SIR system: in the following code, the values of S, I and R are currentS, currentI and currentR. Multiple stages are required to calculate these values for the next time step, which are specified in full detail in Chapter 5 of Volume 1 [BAN 15a].

```
   to calcK [coef]
2    set tmpS currentS + coef * currentKS
     set tmpI currentI + coef * currentKI
     set tmpR currentR + coef * currentKR
     set nextKS (- beta) * tmpI * tmpS
     set nextKI beta * tmpI * tmpS - alpha * tmpI
7    set nextKR alpha * tmpI
   end

   to stepK [coef]
     set nextS nextS + coef * nextKS
12   set nextI nextI + coef * nextKI
     set nextR nextR + coef * nextKR
     set currentKS nextKS
     set currentKI nextKI
     set currentKR nextKR
17 end

   ;; deltaT is the integration step

   to RKstepNetwork
22   (foreach (list 0 (1 / 2) (1 / 2) 1) (list (1 / 6) (1 / 3) (1 / 3) (1 /
        6)) [
      calcK ?1 * deltaT
      stepK ?2 * deltaT
     ])

27     ;; update of the values of currentS, currentI and currentR
       set currentS nextS
       set currentI nextI
       set currentR nextR
   end
```

This same method can be applied to the Metapop model with coupled SIR. We must simply account for inflow and outflow at each of the nodes.

```
to calcK [coef]
  set tmpS currentS + coef * currentKS
  set tmpI currentI + coef * currentKI
4  set tmpR currentR + coef * currentKR
  set nextKS (- beta / (tmpS + tmpI + tmpR)) * tmpI * tmpS
  set nextKI (beta / (tmpS + tmpI + tmpR)) * tmpI * tmpS - alpha * tmpI
  set nextKR alpha * tmpI
  end
9

  to coupling

  ; Outflow = sum of mij for each out-link of the nodes
14  ; this outflow is multiplied by the population of the nodes later

  let sumOutS 0
  let sumOutI 0
  let sumOutR 0
19
    ask my-out-links
    [
      set sumOutS sumOutS + mij
      set sumOutI sumOutI + mij
24    set sumOutR sumOutR + mij
    ]

    ; Inflow : sum of mij * gs * tmpS, mij * gi * tmpI, mij * gr * tmpR for
        each in-link
    ; where tmpS, tmpI and tmpR are the number of S, I, R of the source node
        during the RK4 procedure
29
    let sumInS 0
    let sumInI 0
    let sumInR 0

34  ask in-link-neighbors
    [
      let mi [Mij] of out-link-to myself
      set sumInS sumInS + gs * tmpS * mi
      set sumInI sumInI + gi * tmpI * mi
39    set sumInR sumInR + gr * tmpR * mi
    ]

    ; Update of the number of S, I and R in each node, taking into account
        outflows and inflows

44  set nextKS nextKS - sumOutS * gs * tmpS + sumInS
    set nextKI nextKI - sumOutI * gi * tmpI + sumInI
    set nextKR nextKR - sumOutR * gr * tmpR + sumInR
```

```
     end

49 to stepK [coef]
       set nextS nextS + coef * nextKS
       set nextI nextI + coef * nextKI
       set nextR nextR + coef * nextKR
       set currentKS nextKS
54     set currentKI nextKI
       set currentKR nextKR
     end

     to RKstepNetwork
59   (foreach (list 0 (1 / 2) (1 / 2) 1) (list (1 / 6) (1 / 3) (1 / 3) (1 / 6))
       [
         ask nodes [calcK ?1 * deltaT]
         ask nodes [coupling]
         ask nodes [stepK ?2 * deltaT]
64   ])
       ask nodes
       [
         set currentS nextS
         set currentI nextI
69       set currentR nextR
       ]
     end
```

3.5.3. *Examples of results*

[BAN 15b] presents the results of both models (Metapop and MicMac). We chose the following indicators to analyze these results:

– $MaxI$: the maximum number of infected individuals at any given moment;

– $TimeofMaxI$: the moment at which the maximum number of infected individuals occurred;

– $Duration$: the duration of the epidemic.

This choice of indicators allows us to characterize how the propagation of the disease though the population changes.

The first interesting result is that if we assume that the network is complete, the S, I and R populations and the mobility rates are uniformly distributed over all nodes, and the weights are equal on all edges of the network, then the MetaPop model is equivalent to an SIR system on the total population.

[BAN 15b] also shows the impact of different topologies on the disease spread. In summary, decreasing the diameter and the average length of paths in a network increases the value of $MaxI$ and decreases the values of $TimeofMaxI$ and $Duration$. This is characteristic of an increase in the rate of diffusion of a disease within a population.

3.6. SIR coupling with scaling: MicMac model

The MetaPop model assumes that the population moves instantaneously between cities. We can include this hypothesis in the MicMac model by introducing a new type of agent (typically representing aircraft) that transports individuals between cities. This model therefore introduces a change in scale and a new paradigm, since the epidemiological dynamics of city populations are described by equations, and the epidemiological dynamics between cities are modeled by single agents and their movements.

3.6.1. *Model presentation*

The MicMac model uses the same city agents as above, with the same equation-based epidemiological dynamics (also described by the SIR model). The difference between the 2 models lies in the "mobility" component of the model, which is disaggregated and discrete: individuals are extracted from each city and travel to other cities by airplane. The flight duration depends on the distance, and is adjusted to the integration step. A preliminary calibration phase is performed for each simulation to synchronize the integration step, flight durations and distances, based on the duration of an observed epidemic. The same principle of conservation of population is satisfied: the total population is constant and at any given moment is equal to the sum of the populations in the nodes and in the airplanes.

The interface of this hybrid model is presented in Figure 3.8.

Whereas the Metapop model had instantaneous movements, in the hybrid model the dynamics of the epidemic need to be defined. Indeed, the disease continues to propagate during flights, inside the airplanes. Thus, at each time step, we need to update the number of individuals both in the cities and in the air. For now, we will use an ODE-based SIR model to describe contagion in the air.

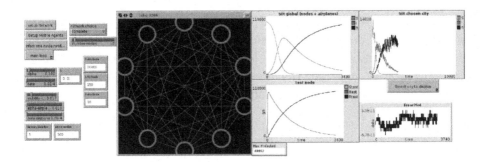

Figure 3.8. *Interface of the hybrid micro-macro model, allowing the user to define the network topology, mobility rates, and initial population distribution. We can observe the dynamics at each node, but also the dynamics of the whole network. At each time step, the difference between the total population in the network and the initial population is calculated to ensure that the total population remains constant while passing from the population to individuals and vice versa*

3.6.2. *General description of the working principle of the coupling*

Figure 3.9 gives a global overview of the dynamics of the MicMac model in the form of an activity diagram. The simulation loop is divided into 4 main stages, each of which has its own method for coupling the equation-based model with the agent-based model.

Firstly, the infectious state of the population in cities (nodes agents) and aircraft (mobilegroup agents) is updated. This dynamic is described by the system of SIR equations. Each step of the simulation corresponds to one integration step of the SIR system: consequently, the numerical solution of the system and the updates of the agent-based model are synchronized. The synchronization begins at model initialization by performing a calibration phase on a test node. The numerical solution is presented in the next section.

Next, new airplanes are created. Each node is assigned a continuous stock of population representing the proportion that desires to leave. Named stock-to-flight, this stock depends in particular on a mobility rate representing the fraction of the total population that can travel by plane at each time step. The stock is incremented at each simulation step. The algorithm creates planes according to the following principle: as many full planes as possible are created at each step of the simulation and each node. Thus, at each simulation step, if the value of stock-to-flight exceeds the capacity of a plane, a plane agent is created with a destination city chosen randomly from the neighbors of the current node, containing a number of passengers equal to its capacity. The population of the aircraft is then extracted from the city of departure. The number of individuals in each state is proportional to the distribution within the city, and is calculated using a lottery algorithm specified in section 3.6.5.2. The number of people in the plane is then subtracted from the stock-to-flight of that node. While this value remains greater than the capacity of one plane, another plane is created by following the steps given above.

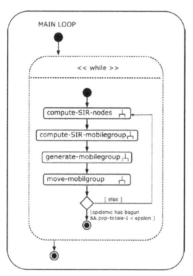

Figure 3.9. *General activity diagram of the MicMac model*

At each step of the simulation, the airplanes travel at a certain speed (and therefore cover a certain distance). This speed is also calibrated at initialization. Once a plane reaches its destination city, its population merges with the global population of the city (see section 3.6.5), and disappears. Thus, if the plane contained infected persons, they could potentially contaminate the population in the destination city, allowing the virus to travel from city to city.

3.6.3. *Initialization: calibrating the model*

At the beginning of the simulation, an SIR model is integrated on a reference node using the parameter values specified by the user. This node contains the total population of the model, and uses the same stopping condition for calibration as the simulation (namely that proportion of infected individuals is below a certain threshold ϵ). The number of iterations of the RK4 method required to achieve this stopping condition is calculated, and the relation between the duration of the epidemic specified by the user and the number of RK4 iterations is calculated to determine the "duration" of each time step. Since the aspect of space is incorporated into the model by specifying the network structure, this preliminary operation allows the size of each edge to be derived, but also determines the traveling speed and therefore the transport time.

3.6.4. *Using the RK4 extension to perform numerical integration*

The SIR equations of this model are numerically integrated using the RK4 extension (see section 1.2.8 of this book), which is recalled directly in the code as follows:

```
set sir rungeKuta:compute-SIR S_Node I_Node R_Node galpha (gbeta / (S_Node
    + I_Node + R_Node)) integrationStep
```

3.6.5. *Switching between the continuous and discrete parts of the model*

The MicMac model associates equation-based dynamics and agent-based dynamics. For the former, integrating the system of equations can produce non-integer values for each population stock. For the latter, by definition, the dynamics are expressed in terms of integer numbers of individuals. The interface between these dynamics therefore requires a method for transitioning between continuous and discrete settings.

3.6.5.1. *Transition from discrete to continuous*

Converting discrete values to continuous values is trivial. Each plane contains an integer number of susceptible, infected and recovered persons. Once it arrives at a city, each plane unloads its passengers, which are added to the city stock for each state.

3.6.5.2. *Transition from continuous to discrete: the lottery algorithm*

The reverse situation arises when a plane is created to travel from one city to another, specifically when calculating its integer number of passengers. At this point, we encounter the following problem: how do we obtain integer numbers of susceptible, infected and recovered populations from three population stocks, represented as continuous values, while conserving the proportions of each stock?

To answer this question, we introduce a so-called "lottery" algorithm. We will present this algorithm here, as it is sufficiently general to be useful for a wide range of different problems. It is based on two subroutines: find-state and generate-passengers.

Given a set of (integer) values representing the number of individuals in each state, find-state randomly chooses a state with probability proportional to the number of individuals in this state. The function returns an integer value representing the selected state, corresponding to the index of the state selected from the list passed as a a parameter.

```
   to-report find-state [#roundedStock]

      let roundedPop sum #roundedStock
 4    let random-value (random roundedPop) + 1

      let state 0
      let step-i 0

 9    if roundedPop > 0 [
        foreach #roundedStock
        [
          if state = 0 [
            set random-value random-value - item step-i #roundedStock
14          ifelse random-value <= 0 [
              set state step-i + 1
            ][
              set step-i step-i + 1
            ]
19        ]
        ]
      ]

      report state
24 end
```

The function `generate-passengers` takes the list of the number of individuals in each possible state (pop) and the number of individuals in the group to be generated (`sample_number`) as parameters. It generates and returns a group of `sample_number` individuals, with the same proportions in each state as pop. This group has an integer number of individuals in each state. The returned population is then removed from the population passed as a parameter. This function takes two preliminary precautions:

– the population passed as a parameter is rounded down to the integer below for each state. This means that if one state has the value of 0.3, it will be rounded down to 0.

– it checks that the population passed as a parameter is larger than the number of agents in the expected output population, after rounding.

The `find-state` function is then called `int(sample_number)` times. Each time that it is called, one individual is extracted from the initial population and added to the population that will be returned. Consequently (because of the `find-state` algorithm), if the number of individuals (in the population passed as a parameter) in a certain state hits 0 at some point during the execution of the algorithm, no further individuals will be drawn in this state.

```
1  to-report generate-passengers [pop sample_number]

     let rounded_pop recompute-rounded-population pop
     let S_pop item 0 rounded_pop
     let I_pop item 1 rounded_pop
6    let R_pop item 2 rounded_pop

     let state 0
     let Si 0
     let Ii 0
11   let Ri 0

         if ((sum rounded_pop) >= int(sample_number))
         [
         ;; One returned state by find-state
16       repeat sample_number
         [
          ;; compute/recompute population at each turn
          set state find-state recompute-rounded-population (list S_pop
             I_pop R_pop)

21       if state = 1 [
```

```
                    set Si Si + 1
                    set S_pop S_pop - 1
                  ]

26                if state = 2 [
                    set Ii Ii + 1
                    set I_pop I_pop - 1
                  ]

31                if state = 3 [
                    set Ri Ri + 1
                    set R_pop R_pop - 1
                  ]
                ]
36          ]

      report (list Si Ii Ri)
      end
```

```
    to-report recompute-rounded-population [pop]
      report (list int(item 0 pop) int(item 1 pop) int(item 2 pop))
    end
```

3.6.6. *Example results*

As above for the MetaPop model, the results are taken from [BAN 15b]. We we will also consider the same indicators as before. Similarly to the MetaPop model, the MicMac model can be equivalently rephrased as a system of SIR ODEs on the total population if we consider the special case of a complete network and uniformly distributed population over each node. The MicMac model also requires the assumption of instantaneous travel between cities (or zero distance between cities).

If we do not assume instantaneous travel or uniform distribution, the model no longer coincides with classical SIR nor MetaPop:

– $MaxI$ of MetaPop $> MaxI$ of MicMac;

– $TimeofMaxI$ of MetaPop $< TimeofMaxI$ of MicMac;

– $Duration$ of MetaPop $< Duration$ of MicMac;

These results show that diffusion unfolds more slowly in the MicMac model. This is in particular because a city with an infected individual will not necessarily infect its neighbors (whereas in the MetaPop model this city would always send at least a small proportion of infected individuals to its neighbors once it becomes infected).

The effect of the network topology on the dynamics of the epidemic, on the other hand, is essentially identical in both MicMac and MetaPop. The difference lies in the previous comment: propagation will be slower in the MicMac model because an infected node does not always infect its neighbors.

3.7. Conclusion and outlook

In a massively connected and highly mobile world, studying the diffusion of epidemics is of great social and scientific value. Modeling not just the spatial but also temporal character of propagation leads us to consider hybrid models. In this chapter, we presented a series of different models. The first of these, the equation-based SIR model, is a macroscopic model based on ordinary differential equations. We used the assumptions of this model as the basis for a second, agent-based model that allows us to reproduce similar behavior under certain conditions (EpiSim). Two approaches were considered to describe diffusion within a network of interconnected cities. The first approach, fully macroscopic, describes the population as a homogeneous group. Flows from one city to another are instantaneous, which excludes temporality or state changes (S, I, R) during travel. The second, hybrid approach views cities as homogeneous groups of individuals but allows for heterogeneity in their movements. It also allows us to include a description of travel times and distances. Control strategies (quarantine, avoidance, risk culture, etc.) can be applied to both of these models (MetaPop and MicMac). All strategies applied to cities at a global scale can be tested with either of these models. However, strategies related to individual choices can only be tested with the MicMac model.

Networking, Networks and Dynamic Graphs

4.1. Networking

Networks cannot be confined within a single field of research. The concepts associated with them have considerably changed over time, and continue to do so today. This makes it difficult to give a single clear definition of a network. Networks are also the location of processes and so are embedded in time, and their structure can change; these are the observations on which our approach is based. Throughout this chapter, we will attempt to shed light on these scientific objects by accepting the bias inherently present in the desire to produce mathematical and computational models for studying networks with NetLogo.

4.1.1. *Networks: a vague, equivocal and often misused concept*

Today, networks often obscure the desire to represent the world in terms of points and the directed and undirected links that express the relationship between them. This graphical representation is easy to understand and has obvious advantages, such as providing a discrete description of the universe, but often acts to hide complexity.

Before we go any further, in the spirit of historicity, it is interesting to examine the etymology of the French word for network (*réseau*) to unravel

Chapter written by Stefan BALEV, Antoine DUTOT and Damien OLIVIER.

how its meaning has shifted over the years, and how entire fields have been built around this concept, both adopting it and adapting it. The origin of *réseau* can be traced back to the Latin word *Retis*, whose influence is still visible in the formal French expression *les rets*, meaning "net". By the 16th Century, this had mutated into the old French word *Resueil*, which would later become *résille*, referring to contemporary women's hairnets [MUS 03]. So, historically, networks encapsulate, imprison and shackle things. In the 17th Century, textile-based metaphors abounded, and the concept of a network was understood to describe the intertwining textile or plant fibers employed by weavers and basket-makers. In [BAK 93], Bakis observes that from the 18th Century onward, the word *réseau* has been used in a number of disciplines in general and scholarly education. The military constructed fortification networks and Cassini's triangulation networks allowed geographical space to be mapped out. Doctors also contributed in the 17th Century by developing the concept of flows in the description of venous systems by Harvey in 1628 [HAR 28, SCU 01]. At this point, networks already conceptually articulate and imprison flows, and serve as the location for dynamics. Diderot, in D'Alembert's Dream, formulates a metaphor that identifies humans with musical instruments. A network becomes a set of vibrating strings, strands capable of developing things, gathered into bundles. This introduces the new dynamic of structure. In the 19th Century, the world becomes intermeshed by communication networks [BER 81]: the telegraph (Chappe, 1794), telephone (Bell, 1876) and all kinds of wireless telegraphy and electromagnetic waves, ultimately resulting in radio (Morse, Edison, Hertz, Tesla, Branly, Popoff, Marconi, Lee de Forest, etc.). Saint Simon, in his desire to philosophically justify the scientific revolution of the 19th Century [MUS 03], recorded his socially oriented political thoughts. His parallel approach led him to develop a philosophy of networks and to propose a generalized vision of networks not limited to their biological or technical aspects, but taking into account their social dimensions, as explained by Lemoigne in [LEM 90].

The 20th Century enriched the concept of networks by introducing graph theory, the origins of which may be traced back to Euler (1735) [EUL 41], although the first paper on graph theory was only published in 1936 by Dénes Köenig [KÖN 90]. Mathematicians, computer scientists and even physicists immediately embraced graphs as objects and developed a theoretical background based on an algebraic formalism. Ford and Fulkerson, for example, studied flows in graphs [FOR 11], and Paul Erdös and Alfréd

Rényi proposed a model for random graphs in 1959 [ERD 59] that provides a powerful paradigm for studying properties such as degree distributions and connectivity, as well as path-finding and diffusion mechanisms, among other examples. Since then, new models that better represent the complex types of networks observed in reality have emerged, such as small-world networks based on the works of Watts and Strogatz [WAT 98], and scale-invariant graphs[1], proposed by Barabàsi and Albert [BAR 99].

4.1.2. *From reality to theory*

Mathematically formulating the concept of a network naturally leads to graphs, which are both mathematical and computational objects that describe problems composed of a set of objects and the connections between them.

The elements modeled by the graph are called *vertices* (singular *vertex*)[2], and the relationships between these nodes are called *arrows* or *edges*, depending on whether or not a direction is specified. Thus, a network is a graph whose nodes and links have quantitative or qualitative properties, or in other words signified content [SAU 93]. If these relationships have a direction, we describe the graph as a *directed graph* or *digraph*. So, for a graph G, we write $G = (V, E)$ where V is the set of vertices of the graph and E is the set of edges (or arrows in the case of a directed graph). Some problems require us to assign weights to the vertices and/or edges of a graph. If the elements of a graph have weights, we say that it is a weighted graph, and can optionally further specify whether the weights are attached to vertices, edges or both. Thus, a weighted graph is written as $G = (V, E, p_V, p_E)$ where p_V is a function from $V \rightarrow \mathbf{R}$ and p_E is a function from $E \rightarrow \mathbf{R}$, representing the weights of the vertices and those of the arrows or edges, respectively.

More generally, we might wish to assign more than one value to the elements of a graph. These values, which we will refer to as attributes, can be used to characterize the elements. To do this, we relate an identifier, the *key*, to its corresponding value. If the sets K_V and K_E are the set of possible keys

---

1 Scale-free.

2 *"Nodes"* is also used.

for the nodes and arrows/edges, we can generalize the functions p_V and p_E given above:

$$\begin{cases} p_V : V \times K_V \to \mathbf{R} \\ p_E : E \times K_E \to \mathbf{R} \end{cases}$$

Graph theory is a particularly broad and highly researched field, and would be difficult to present in any level of comprehensiveness within these chapters. The concepts of paths and connectivity are particularly important. Problems can often be reduced to questions about graph searches, which, for example, allow us to determine whether two vertices can be reached, or to characterize the set of vertices that may be reached by starting from a given vertex. The notion of length will often be useful.

In a graph, it is quite natural to move from vertex to vertex along the arrows or edges, and this is precisely what our NetLogo turtles do. These movements generate a path.

DEFINITION 4.1.– *Let $G = (V, E)$ be an undirected graph, and let $a = \{v_i, v_j\} \in E$ be one of its edges. The vertices v_i and v_j are said to be* adjacent, *and the edge a is* incident *to the vertices v_i and v_j. The number of edges incident to v_i is the* degree *of v_i, written as $deg(v_i)$. Two edges are* adjacent *if they share at least one vertex. A graph is said to be* complete *if all vertices are adjacent.*

These definitions can be extended to directed graphs, in which case we speak of the outdegree $(deg_+(v_i))$ and the indegree $(deg_-(v_i))$ of a vertex v to denote the number of arrows leaving and entering v.

DEFINITION 4.2.– *Let $G = (V, E)$ be an undirected graph. A path* of length $k \geq 1$ is an ordered sequence $(e_1, \ldots, e_k)$ of k adjacent edges.

We are often interested in determining whether a path exists, which leads to the notion of connectivity.

DEFINITION 4.3.– *Let $G = (V, E)$ be an undirected graph. The graph G is* connected *if for any pair of vertices (v_i, v_j) there exists a path between them.*

Not every graph is connected, in which case we might wish to determine the maximal connected subgraph, which is one of the graph's connected components.

DEFINITION 4.4.– *Let* $G = (V, E)$ *be an undirected graph. A* connected component C *of this graph is a maximal subset of vertices such that:*

– *if* $v_i \in C$, $\forall v_j \in C$, $i \neq j$, *then there exists a path between* v_i *and* v_j;

– *if* $v_i \in C$, $\forall v_k \in V \setminus C$, *then there does not exist a path bewteen* v_i *and* v_k.

It is clear that a graph is connected if and only if it has a single connected component, and also if the connected components of the graph partition the set of vertices.

Readers who wish to learn more about graph theory can refer to [BON 76]. This book has been around for some time, but is still viewed as a reference on the subject. It presents a comprehensive overview of graph theory and is aimed at a wide audience of both novices and experienced readers.

4.2. Networks and graphs in NetLogo

NetLogo graphs are usually created using the `turtles` and `links` objects. The links are the arrows or edges, and the turtles are the vertices. The basic primitives in NetLogo are `create-link-with`, `create-link-to`, `create-link-from`. The first of these creates an edge between the selected turtle and another turtle. The other two create an arrow from the selected turtle to another turtle, or vice versa.

In the following sections, we will illustrate our discussion by introducing a way to generate random graphs in order to showcase the possibilities offered by NetLogo. Random graphs are the result of simple processes that fix the number of vertices and then randomly add edges. They have been studied in depth by Paul Erdős and Alfred Rényi [ERD 59], and also by Edgar Nelson Gilbert [GIL 59]. They are often used as reference graphs with a fixed number of edges and vertices that can be proven to have certain properties. For example, there exist theoretical results on the size of the largest connected component, and on the distribution of the degrees of the vertices. They also act as unstructured reference graphs for detecting communities[3] using modularity,

---

3 A set of vertices more strongly connected among themselves than with the other vertices of the graph.

which is defined as the difference between the edge density of communities and the average edge density in a random graph [NEW 04].

There are two principal methods for generating random graphs, based on either the works of Erdős-Rényi, or those of Gilbert. To generate a random graph, Erdős and Rényi considered the set $\mathcal{G}_{n,m}$ of all graphs with n vertices and m edges and chose one graph, denoted by $G(n, m)$, from this set. In other words, they randomly chose a subset of m edges from the $\frac{n(n-1)}{2}$ edges of the complete graph, with equal probability. Gilbert proposed another method that revolves around the existence or absence of edges. Edges follow a Bernouilli distribution $\mathbb{P}(X = x) = p^x(1 - p)^{1-x}1_{\{0,1\}}(x)$ with parameter p. Hence, each edge v_i, v_j exists with probability p. Depending on the value of p, this results in very different behavior in the generated graph. Let $G(n, p)$ be one such graph. It has the following properties:

The average number of edges is $\overline{m} = p\frac{n(n-1)}{2}$.

The average vertex degree is pn.

As the number of vertices n tends to infinity:

– if $p < \frac{1}{n}$, there is high probability that the size of the largest connected component is of order $O(\ln n)$. This is the subcritical case;

– if $p = \frac{1}{n}$, there is high probability that the size of the largest connected component is of order $O(n^{2/3})$. This is the critical case;

– if $p > \frac{1}{n}$, there is high probability that the size of the largest connected component is of order $O(n)$. This is the supercritical case.

These $G(n, p)$ graphs have similar properties to Erdős-Rényi graphs when the average number m of edges of $G(n, p)$ is equal to that of $G(n, m)$.

We will now use NetLogo to illustrate some of these properties.

4.2.1. *Generating a random graph*

To create a random graph, we will use the method proposed by Gilbert. We therefore begin by creating the set of vertices, then connect them together with probability $Prob$ (see listing 4.4 line 12). To do this, for a given turtle, we consider all turtles with a greater identifier (who, see Program 4.4 line 11), since our edges are undirected.

The world is configured as follows:

Location of origin	Center
max-pxcor	100
max-pycor	100
world wrap horizontally	☐
world wrap vertically	☐
Patch size	4
view update	on ticks

```
    globals [ MaxDegree ]

    to setup
      ca ; Clean up
 5    create-turtles NumberOfNodes [
        set shape "circle" ; To represent nodes
        set size 2
        setxy random-xcor random-ycor ; We randomly position them somewhere
      ]
10    ask turtles [ ; Consider each turtle
        ask other turtles with [who > [who] of myself][ ; This ensures that we
            only consider each node once
          if random-float 1.0 < Prob  ; Connections exist with a certain
              probability
          [
            create-link-with myself
15        ]
        ]
      ]
      set MaxDegree max [count link-neighbors] of turtles
      reset-ticks
20  end

    to display-graph
    repeat 3 [
      layout-spring (turtles with [any? link-neighbors]) links SpringResistance
          ReposLength Repulsion
25    display
    ]
    end
```

Listing 4.1. *Generating a random graph*

We add a display function that will allow us to prepare the graph for presentation (layout-spring). It uses an algorithm based on physical forces, viewing each edge as a spring [TUT 63]. At each iteration, the algorithm calculates the sum of the forces applied to each of the vertices, then moves them until a stable state is found. The interface of our simulation is completed by adding two curves that plot the distribution of the degrees, with linear and logarithmic scales.

```
     ;; Plot setup commands
     plot-pen-reset
3    set-plot-x-range 0 MaxDegree + 1

     ;; Plot update commands
     histogram [count link-neighbors] of turtles
```

Listing 4.2. *Distribution of degrees with linear scale*

```
     ;; Plot setup commands
     plot-pen-reset
     set-plot-x-range 0 log (MaxDegree + 1) 10
4
     ;; Plot update commands
     let degree 1 ; To avoid log(0)
     while [degree <= MaxDegree] [
       let nb count turtles with [count link-neighbors = degree]
9    if nb > 0
         [ plotxy log degree 10
                  log nb 10 ]
       set degree degree + 1
     ]
```

Listing 4.3. *Distribution of degrees with logarithmic scale*

We also add four monitors to the user interface (Figure 4.1), which will allow us to compare the theoretical results with the experimental results.

4.2.2. *Search for the largest connected component*

To find the largest connected component, we need to determine the set of components. This will require us to visit each of the vertices in the graph. They are initially all marked as unvisited (set visited? false) and are set to visited when they are considered (set visited? true). To implement the process, we choose an unvisited vertex and explore the graph from this vertex, either depth-first or breadth-first. If we have visited the entire graph from the first vertex, then the graph is connected; otherwise we have simply characterized one connected component. In this case, we simply choose another unvisited vertex and repeat the process. To complete the proposed code (listing 4.4), we add two global variables, which remember the starting vertex of the largest known connected component RootLargestComponent and its size SizeLargestcomponent. Each turtle representing a vertex is assigned a variable that records whether or not it has been visited (visited?).

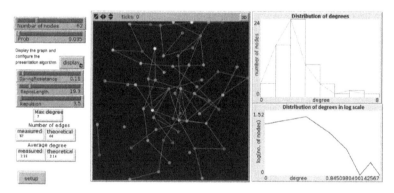

Figure 4.1. *Random graph with its degree distribution, average degree (theoretical and measured) and the number of edges. For a color version of the figure, see www.iste.co.uk/banos/netlogo2.zip*

```
    globals
    [
      MaxDegree ; Maximum vertex degree encountered
      SizeLargestComponent ; Size of the largest connected component
5     SizeLargestTheoComponent
      RootLargestComponent ; Vertex belonging to the largest connected
            component so that we can display it
    ]

    turtles-own [ visited? ]
10
    to setup
      ;; Reuse the code from Listing 4.4
      ;; and add
      determine-connected-components
15
```

```
     reset-ticks
     end

     to determine-connected-components
20   set SizeLargestComponent 0
     let graphExplored? false
     while [ not graphExplored? ] ; While the graph has not yet been fully
         explored
     [
     let componentRoot one-of turtles with [ not visited? ]
25   ifelse componentRoot = nobody
     [
       set graphExplored? true
     ]
     [
30     let sizeComponent 0
       ask rootComponent [ set sizeComponent path-width ]
       if sizeComponent > SizeLargestComponent
       [
         set SizeLargestComponent sizeComponent
35       set RootLargestComponent rootComponent
       ]
     ]
     ]
     show-largest-component
40 end

     to-report path-width
     let size 1
     let queue (list self)
45   let node self
     let neighbor []
     set visited? true
     while [ not empty? queue ]
     [
50     set node first queue
       set queue butfirst queue
       ask node [
         set color yellow
         set neighbor link-neighbors with [ not visited? ]
55       if any? neighbor [
           set queue sentence queue neighbor
           ask neighbor [ set visited? true ]
           set size size + count neighbor
         ]
60     ]
     ]
     report size
     end

65 to show-largest-component
     let x 0
     ask turtles [ set visited? false ]
     ask RootLargestComponent [ set x path-width ]
```

```
        ask turtles with [visited? ]
70      [
          set color green
          ask my-links [ set color green
          set thickness 0.7
          ]
75      ]
      end
```

Listing 4.4. *Searching for connected components*

We can now compare the theoretical results (see section 4.2) with the experimental results obtained by simulation (see Figure 4.2). We calculate the size of the largest connected component using the function calculate-size-largest-component (see listing 4.5).

```
    to calculate-size-largest-component
      ifelse Prob < 1 / NumberOfNodes
3     [
        set SizeLargestTheoComponent ln NumberOfNodes
        output-print "Subcritical"
      ]
      [
8       ifelse Prob = 1 / NumberOfNodes
        [set SizeLargestTheoComponent NumberOfNodes ^ (2. / 3) output-print
            "Critical"]
        [set SizeLargestTheoComponent NumberOfNodes output-print
            "Supercritical"]
      ]
    end
```

Listing 4.5. *Theoretically determining the size of the largest connected component*

4.2.3. *Searching for the shortest path*

Searching for the shortest path according to a given metric is a classical problem that we often encounter while traveling. Software using satellite geopositioning attempts to provide somewhat sophisticated assistance in this task, and relies on classical algorithms from graph theory. We will present Dijkstra's algorithm [DIJ 71], which allows us to determine the shortest path between a start vertex and an end vertex in a graph weighted by positive real numbers. These real numbers could represent, for example, time, distance or traffic lights.

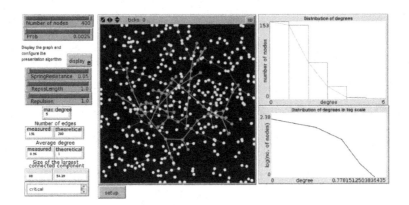

Figure 4.2. *Random graph and its largest component. For a color version of the figure, see www.iste.co.uk/banos/netlogo2.zip*

The example that we will consider was taken from the French Baccalaureate examination in 2009 [NAT 09]. Consider the graph shown in Figure 4.3, where the vertex A represents the location of maintenance services, and B, C, D, E, F and G represent the locations of public parks. Roads connecting two locations are represented by edges weighted by the number of traffic lights present on each road. The following problem was posed: "Determine the path with the fewest traffic lights between A and G. Your answer should be justified by specifying an algorithm."

One of the possible answers to this examination question is Dijkstra's algorithm.

As an input, the algorithm takes a weighted graph $G = (V, E, p_E)$ where p_E is a function from $V \rightarrow \mathbf{R}^+$. The algorithm works with both directed and undirected graphs. It can also be applied to unweighted graphs by simply taking the function $p_E \rightarrow \{1\}$. We begin by choosing a start node, which in our case is A, and then construct a subgraph in which the vertices are placed in increasing order with respect to the distance calculated from the start vertex. The distance is the sum of the weights of the edges traversed. The algorithm performs the following steps:

1) Assign a value to each vertex of the graph, 0 for the start vertex, ∞ for the other vertices.

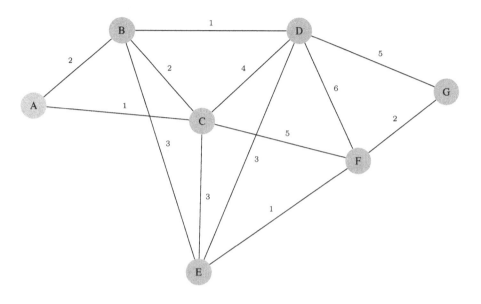

Figure 4.3. *Roads connecting public parks and the maintenance services at A. The numbers on each edge indicate the number of traffic lights [NAT 09]*

2) Choose the current vertex to be the start vertex. Mark this vertex as visited, all other vertices as unvisited and add them to the set of visitable vertices.

3) From the current vertex, find the set of unvisited neighbors. For each element in this set, calculate the hypothetical distance if this element were to be chosen. Compare this new value with the value previously assigned to the vertex, and reassign the smallest of the two to this vertex.

4) Mark the current vertex as visited, and remove it from the set of visitable vertices.

5) If the target vertex has been marked as visited, a solution has been found. If the set of visitable vertices only contains vertices with the value ∞, then there does not exist a path between the start vertex and the end vertex. Otherwise, choose the unvisited node with the smallest assigned value, and return to step 3.

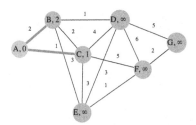

a) We start from node A. Update the neighbors of A, which are B and C. Their assigned values become 2 and 1, whereas the other nodes keep the value ∞.

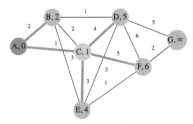

b) C is chosen, and we update its neighbors D, E and F. B does not change, as its value is smaller.

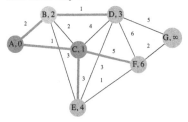

c) B is chosen, and we update its neighbor D.

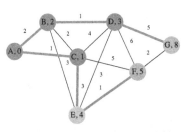

d) D is chosen, and we update its neighbor G.

e) E is chosen, and we update its neighbor F.   f) F is chosen, and we update its neighbor G.

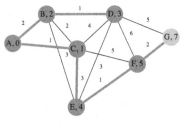

g) G is chosen, and we have finished constructing the subgraph. The path $ACEFG$ has the fewest traffic lights (7).

Figure 4.4. *Executing Dijkstra's algorithm*

To begin, we must first create the graph based on the one shown in Figure 4.3. We define a breed of turtle to represent the nodes of the graph: breed [nodes node]. To each turtle with this specific breed, we assign the information nodes-own [myName]. In this version of the implementation, only the name of the node is saved. The edges of the graph are represented as undirected links by NetLogo, and we will use a specific breed: undirected-link-breed [edges edge] to which we assign the edge weight edges-own [weight]. One turtle of type nodeName is assigned to each node, so that we can position the name at the desired location, which is managed by the methods create-name [which] (see listing 4.6, line 64) and reposition-name [angle dep] (see listing 4.6, line 76). Nodes and edges are created with the methods setup-nodes (see listing 4.6, line 21) and setup-edges (see listing 4.6, line 42). Nodes are created from a string of characters representing the set of names and a list of positions. We first create the nodes and then list them in order so that we can set each of their positions. The edges are created using the list edgesOfGraph, which represents edges as lists [head tail weight].

```
   breed [ nodes node ] ; The nodes of the graph
   nodes-own [ myName ] ; Information attached to each node (its name)

   undirected-link-breed [ edges edge ] ; The edges of the graph
 5 edges-own [ weight ] ; The weights of the edges

   breed [ names name ] ; To properly handle the information attached to the
       nodes
   directed-link-breed [ nodeNames nodeName ] ; Links connecting the turtle
       nodes and the turtle names

10 ;================================================================================
   ;
   ; Initialization
   ;
   ;================================================================================
15 to setup ; The usual function
     ca
     setup-nodes
     setup-edges
   end
20
   to setup-nodes ; Initialize the graph nodes
     let string "ABCDEFG" ; Set the node names
     let positions [[1 5.5] [4 8] [6.7 5] [10 8] [6.6 0] [12 3.7] [15 6]]
                              ; Position of nodes
25   create-nodes 7 [
```

```
         set shape "circle 2"
         set color 7
         set size 3
         set heading 0
30   ]
     foreach sort nodes ; List them in order so that the nodes are correctly
         positioned
     [ ask ? ; relative to the list of positions
       [
         setxy ((first first positions) * 2 + size) ((last first positions) *
             2 + size)
35       set positions but-first positions
         set myName substring String (who) (who + 1)
         create-name myName ; Create a name associated with the node
       ]
     ]
40   end

     to setup-edges ; Initialize the graph edges
       let edgesOfGraph [["A" "B" 2] ["A" "C" 1] ["B" "C" 2] ["B" "D" 1] ["B"
           "E" 3]
                        ["C" "D" 4] ["C" "E" 3] ["C" "F" 5] ["D" "E" 3] ["D"
                            "F" 6]
45                      ["D" "G" 5] ["E" "F" 1] ["F" "G" 2]] ; The edges and
                            their weights
       foreach edgesOfGraph ; Iterate through the list of graph edges
       [
         ask nodes with [myName = first ?] ; Start node
         [
50         create-edge-with one-of nodes with [myName = item 1 ?] ; Create the
               edge with the end node
           [
             set weight item 2 ? ; Set the weight of the edge
             set label weight ; Display the weight of the edge in the graph
           ]
55       ]
       ]
     end


     ;===========================================================================
60   ;
     ; Useful functions
     ;
     ;===========================================================================
     to create-name [ which ]
65     hatch-names 1 [ ; Each turtle node creates a turtle name
         set size 0
         set label which
         create-nodeName-from myself [ ; Create a link with the node
           tie ; Link them together
70         hide-link
         ]
         reposition-name 160 0.5 ; Reposition so that the label of the name
       ] ; is in the middle of the node
```

```
   end
75
   to reposition-name [ angle dep ]
     move-to one-of in-nodeName-neighbors
     set heading angle
     fd dep
80 end
```

Listing 4.6. *Dijkstra's algorithm applied to the French*
Baccalaureate problem: creating a graph [NAT 09]

To implement Dijkstra's algorithm, we will first complete the initialization phase. We need to fix the start node and the node that we are attempting to reach. We also need to store the cost of the best path found so far to reach each node in that node. Initially, the cost is infinite for nodes that have not yet been visited. For the start node, it is zero. We will complete the listing 4.6 by adding or modifying the elements in listing 4.7.

```
   ; Reuse listing 4.6.
   globals [
     StartNode
     EndNode
 5   CurrentNode
     Infinity
   ]

   nodes-own [ myName value visited? predecessor ] ; Information attached to
       each node
10
   ;==============================================================================
   ;
   ; Initialization
   ;
15 ;==============================================================================
   to setup ; The usual function
     ca
     setup-nodes
     setup-edges
20   setup-dijkstra
   end

   to setup-dijkstra
     set Infinity 1E50
25   ask nodes [ ; Vertices that have not yet been visited
       set value Infinity ; Set to infinity
       set visited? false ; Unvisited
       set predecessor nobody ; No predecessor is known
     ]
30   set StartNode one-of nodes with [myName = "A"] ; Define the start node
```

```
     set EndNode one-of nodes with [myName = "G"] ; Define the node we are
         trying to reach
     ask StartNode [
       set color pink
       set value 0
35   ]
     ask EndNode [ set color pink ]
     set CurrentNode StartNode ; Used to search the graph
   end
```

Listing 4.7. *Dijkstra's algorithm applied to the French Baccalaureate problem: initialization [NAT 09]*

We now need to write the algorithm described above in section 4.2.3. The dijkstra method is the general method that selects the current vertex and the update-neighbors method finds the set of unvisited neighbors and calculates the distance required to reach it given the current path: if the result is smaller, then it is saved.

```
1
   ;============================================================================
   ;
   ; Dijkstra's algorithm
   ;
6  ;============================================================================
   to dijkstra
     ifelse CurrentNode != EndNode and CurrentNode != nobody ; There exists a
         current node
     [ ; and the algorithm has not terminated
       ask CurrentNode [
11       update-neighbors ; Update neighbors if necessary
         set color 3
         set visited? true
       ]
       set CurrentNode min-one-of ( nodes with [ not visited? and value <
           Infinity ]) [ value ]
16     ; Select the node with the smallest value as the current node
     ]
     [
       ifelse ( CurrentNode = nobody) ; No path?
       [output-print (word "No path between vertices " [myName] of StartNode "
           and " [myName] of EndNode) ]
21     [
         ask CurrentNode ; The current node is the destination
         [ set color 3
           set visited? true
         ]
26     ]
       stop
```

```
      ]
   end

31 to update-neighbors
      ask edge-neighbors with [ not visited? ] ; Consider unvisited nodes
      [ ; Calculate their values with the chosen paths
        let newValue [ value ] of CurrentNode + [ weight ] of edge-with
            CurrentNode
        if newValue < value ; If the path is better than the previous path
36      [ ; Update
          set value newValue ; the value and the predecessor
          if predecessor != nobody [ ask edge-with predecessor [ set thickness
              0.1 ]]
          ask edge-with CurrentNode [ set thickness 0.4 ]
          set predecessor myself
41        ask out-nodeName-neighbors [ set label (word [ myName ] of myself " "
              newValue ) reposition-name 140 0.8 ]
        ]
      ]
   end
```

Listing 4.8. *Dijkstra's algorithm applied to the*
French Baccalaureate problem: searching [NAT 09]

On the user interface, (see Figure 4.5), three buttons have been created. The first creates the graph, the second executes the algorithm step-by-step, and the last runs the full algorithm. An output window has also been added to indicate if there is no path.

4.2.4. *Modularity metric*

When studying graphs and networks, we encounter many examples of graphs arising from both physical and virtual processes that are structured into *communities*. These communities may be informally described as groups of vertices in the graph that are more densely interconnected with each other than with the rest of the graph (Figure 4.6). The term community is used when considering graphs from a synchronic perspective, and the term *organization* is used from a diachronic perspective when studying the evolution of the topology of a graph or a network.

Being able to detect these communities will allow us to better apprehend, understand and represent the structure of the graph. In some graphs, for example based on social networks or simulated networks of interactions, the goal is to identify existing, known communities. However, in most cases, our objective will be to determine whether any such structures exist. We therefore need an indicator to measure the relevance of the communities that we find.

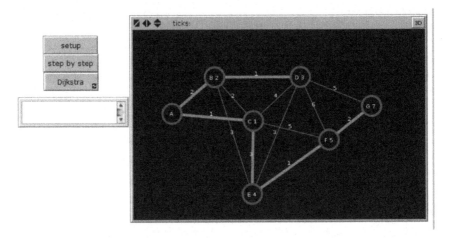

Figure 4.5. *NetLogo interface of the program searching for the shortest path in a graph using Dijkstra's algorithm*

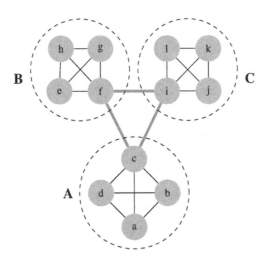

Figure 4.6. *Example of communities within a graph. The three groups of vertices with dotted lines are more interconnected among themselves than with the rest of the graph*

There are several possible ways of measuring this, but the one that has proven most useful is the *modularity* metric introduced by Newman and Girvan [NEW 04, NEW 06]. The basic idea of this metric is, for a given partition into communities, to compare the proportion of intracommunity connections after subtracting the value that this quantity takes in an identical graph with randomly distributed connections.

To make this idea precise, for a graph with a given partition into k communities, we define the symmetric $k \times k$ matrix e, whose entries $e_{i,j}$ are given by the proportion of connections between community i and community j, such that the sum $||e||$ of all entries of the matrix is equal to 1. Here is matrix e for the example in Figure 4.6:

$$\mathbf{e} = \begin{pmatrix} \frac{12}{42} & \frac{1}{42} & \frac{1}{42} \\ \frac{1}{42} & \frac{12}{42} & \frac{1}{42} \\ \frac{1}{42} & \frac{1}{42} & \frac{12}{42} \end{pmatrix}$$

In order to be able to apply this concept to directed graphs, we count the "starting points" of connections rather than the connections themselves. Thus, within community A, we have 12 starting points, one of which goes to community B and another of which goes to community C.

The trace of this matrix $Tr\mathbf{e} = \sum_u e_{ii}$ therefore gives the proportion of intercommunity connections in the graph. If the value of the trace is high, we can deduce that community structures are strongly present. But this is not enough, as we could achieve the maximum value for the trace, which is 1, simply by defining one single community.

The sum of the rows of the matrix $a_i = \sum_j e_{ij}$ is the proportion of total connections of a community i. If all of the connections of a graph are uniformly distributed over the vertices, we would have $e_{ij} = a_i a_j$. We can use this model as a reference graph for comparison.

Thus, to compare the proportion of intracommunity connections to this same proportion in a graph with random connections, we can write the modularity:

$$Q = \sum_i (e_{ii} - a_{ij}^2) = Tr\mathbf{e} - ||e^2||$$

For values close to $Q = 0$, the connections will be distributed almost randomly, whereas for values close to the maximum value of $Q = 1$, community structures will be strongly present.

One broad class of community-searching methods uses the technique of hierarchically subdividing graphs and then calculating the modularity of these divisions. The peak values yield the best partitions. One of the easiest approaches to implement in NetLogo is a method that removes connections judged to be likely to lie between communities, allowing us to identify communities as connected components.

The intuition behind these methods is that within a community, there will be many paths between vertices. But if the graph is very modular, there will be some small set of unavoidable connections between communities. One typical example of this kind of connection is given by *articulation points*, which are connections through which every path between pairs of distinct vertices must necessarily pass.

The betweenness centrality [BRA 01, GIR 02] of a connection is the number of shortest paths between each pair of vertices that must pass through this connection. We now have $O(nm)$ algorithms to calculate this value, where m is the number of connections and n is the number of vertices. One such algorithm is included in the NetLogo Network extension, which we will use here.

In the next section, we will implement a method for dividing graphs that works as follows:

1) Calculate the betweenness centrality of each connection.

2) Remove the connection with the highest value.

3) Find the connected components and consider each of them as a distinct community.

4) Calculate the modularity of the original graph with these communities (note that the modularity must be calculated with the original graph, before removing connections).

5) Return to step 1 until each vertex belongs to some community.

At the end of this process, the partition with the highest modularity is chosen as the solution.

To do this, we will need to define a graph, calculate the betweenness centrality and finally implement a procedure for calculating the modularity. The first two tasks can be achieved with the Network extension of NetLogo, which we load in the very first line:

```
1  extensions [ nw ]

   globals [
     ; Modularity depends on how the communities are arranged.
     modularity
6    ; Number of edges in the graph.
     m
     ; Current number of communities.
     components
   ]
11
   ; Breeds specific to internal community links...
   undirected-link-breed [ internal-links internal-link ]
   ; ... or external community links.
   undirected-link-breed [ external-links external-link ]
16 ; The links remember their centrality.
   internal-links-own [ centrality ]
```

Listing 4.9. *Optimizing the modularity, step 1: definitions*

We will use global variables to store the value of the modularity while it is being calculated, the number of connections in the graph, and each of the communities corresponding to some connected component of the graph as we gradually remove connections. This will be a set of agentsets containing the vertices of each community.

To identify the communities by finding connected components, we will need a graph from which the connections have already been removed. However, the modularity must be calculated on the original graph. We will therefore introduce two species for links, named internal-links and external-links, which, as their names suggest, represent intracommunity links and intercommunity links, respectively. The internal links store the value of the centrality.

```
   to setup
     ca
3    ; In the network extension, all of the turtles are vertices of the graph
     ; but the edges belong to the breed "internal-links".
     nw:set-context turtles internal-links
     set components 1
     set-default-shape turtles "circle"
8    load-graph
     set m count links
     reset-ticks
   end

13 ; Load and initialize a graph.
   to load-graph
     ; Load the graph in GraphML format
     nw:load-graphml "test.graphml"
     ; Calculate the initial centrality.
18   betweenness
     ; Format the graph with an algorithm based on forces.
     repeat 5000 [ layout-spring turtles links 0.2 5 1 ]
     ask turtles [ set color red ]
   end
```

Listing 4.10. *Optimizing the modularity, step 2: initialization*

The initialization procedure tells the Network extension which breeds of turtle will represent the vertices of the graph (in this case, all turtles), and which breed of links will represent the connections (in this case, only intracommunity links). This will allow us to calculate the betweenness centrality on the modified graph.

To avoid complicating the program, we will assume that the loaded graph only has one single connected component.

The load-graph procedure uses the Network extension to load a graph by creating a turtle for each vertex and a link for each connection. The procedure then initializes each link with a centrality value, and formats the graph to improve its readability. In the following, we use the graph from Figure 4.6.

```
   ; Calculate the betweenness centrality for each vertex of type
       "internal-link".
   to betweenness
3    ; Assign the value of the betweenness centrality to each internal link of
       the graph, and display it.
```

```
     ask internal-links [
       set centrality nw:betweenness-centrality
       set label precision centrality 1
       set color 9.99999
  8  ]
     end
```

Listing 4.11. *Optimizing the modularity, step 3: betweenness centrality*

The betweenness method from the Network extension calculates the centrality at each connection, and displays it.

```
  1  Find the next possible community.
     to next-communities
       ; Find the graph link(s) with the highest centrality.
       let ml internal-links with-max [ centrality ]
       ; Transform these links into external links.
  6    ask one-of ml [ set breed external-links set color 12 set label "" ]
       ; Calculate the connected components based on the remaining internal
           links,
       ; which tells us the communities (in the form of a list of agentsets).
       let communities nw:weak-component-clusters
       ; If there is a new component...
  11   if length communities > components [
         set components length communities
         ; Assign a random color to each community.
         foreach communities [
           let clr one-of base-colors ; (item (i mod 14) base-colors)
  16       ask ? [ set color clr ]
         ]
         ; Recalculate the modularity.
         compute-modularity communities
         tick
  21   ]
       ; Recalculate the "betweenness" using only the remaining internal links.
       betweenness
     end
```

Listing 4.12. *Optimizing the modularity, step 4: finding communities*

The next-communities method is tasked with finding the link(s) with maximal centrality, and randomly selecting one of them to convert to the external-links breed, the group of links between communities. For example, we will use the Network extension to identify the connected components due to nw:weak-component-clusters, which returns a set of `agentsets`, one for each community. This set is stored in the global `communities` variable, which we will later use to calculate the modularity.

If the number of components has changed, i.e. if we have found a new partition of the graph into communities, we assign them colors for readability, and then recalculate the betweenness centrality.

We can repeatedly call this procedure to determine the successive partitions of the graph into communities. After doing this, we need to calculate the value of the modularity for each new partition. The best partition is the one with the highest modularity.

To calculate this, we could directly introduce the matrix e, but in NetLogo this would require another extension. There is another way to calculate the modularity that is better suited to NetLogo, by iterating over each community, since:

$$Q = \sum_i (e_{ii} - a_{ij}^2)$$

The following procedure implements this formulation:

```
1  ; Calculate the modularity over all communities passed as arguments.
   to compute-modularity [ communities ]
     set modularity 0
     foreach communities [
       ; The current community is i.
6      let i ?
       ; Proportion of edges with both vertices in community i.
       let eii 0
       ; Proportion of edge end points attached to a vertex in i.
       let ai 0
11     ; Shortcut for 2 * m. 2 * m since we are counting edge start points.
       let m2 (2 * m)
       ; For each vertex in i.
       ask i [
         set ai (ai + (( count link-neighbors ) / m2))
16       ; For each internal links in i.
         ask link-neighbors [
           if member? self i [ set eii (eii + (1 / m2)) ]
         ]
       ]
```

```
21      set modularity (modularity + (eii - (ai * ai)))
      ]
      show components
      show modularity
   end
```

Listing 4.13. *Optimizing the modularity, step 5: calculating the modularity*

Thus, `compute-modularity` iterates through the set of communities calculated by `next-communities`, and determines in each case the value e_{ii} of the proportion of intracommunity connections, and a_i the proportion of all connections within the community. It then updates the value of `modularity` by incrementing in the calculation corresponding to the current community.

Our final task is to set up the graphical interface. We propose creating a button for initialization, and another for switching between partitions into communities. Finally, including a graph will allow us to observe the evolution of the modularity value. Figure 4.7 shows the result and the modularity calculation.

4.2.5. *Communities*

Other than the method that we just presented, there are a large number of other algorithms for finding community structures in graphs. Interested readers can refer to Fortunato [FOR 10] for a relatively comprehensive overview of this topic. The method that we propose to implement here uses the propagation of information within the graph, and is particularly well adapted to NetLogo.

The algorithm was suggested by Raghavan, Albert and Kumara [RAG 07]. The central idea is to allow labels to diffuse throughout the graph. These labels will then be used to identify the communities. The advantage of this algorithm is that it is directly "agentifiable": the decisions are made individually by each turtle-node agent of the graph based on its neighborhood. Hence, no global knowledge of the state of the graph is required. Another important advantage of this algorithm is its speed, as it runs in almost linear time. Finally, the algorithm does not require an objective function like the modularity, although the quality of the partitions may of course be improved by considering one.

Unlike the previous method, this method is constructive. We start with a set of nodes, each of which has a different label. We will use the unique NetLogo identifier of each turtle. Each agent then iteratively selects a new label as a function of the most common label in its immediate neighborhood, i.e. the vertices to which it is directly connected by an arrow or an edge. The algorithm terminates when a consensus is reached, i.e. when the labels no longer change.

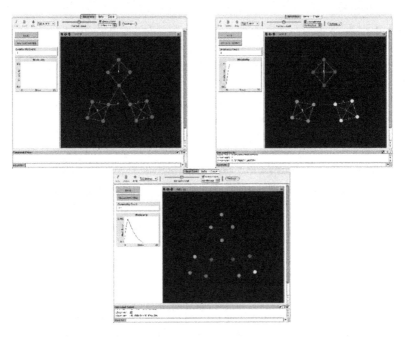

Figure 4.7. *Setting up the graphical interface to calculate the modularity. For a color version of the figure, see www.iste.co.uk/banos/netlogo2.zip*

The update process can be synchronous, with all agents updating themselves based on their neighbors in the previous step, or asynchronous, in which case all agents update themselves based on the current state of their neighbors, which may have changed since the beginning of the iteration. The latter technique is more suitable for NetLogo, and so this is the one that we chose to implement.

Here are the steps of the algorithm:

1) Assign a unique label to each vertex.

2) Iterate over each vertex (in random order) and ask it to choose the dominant label in its neighborhood.

3) Repeat step 2 until a consensus is reached, i.e. no label changes.

```
     extensions [ nw table ]

     globals [
       ; Current number of communities.
5    components
       ; Table relating each known tag to a usage counter.
       ; Each tag represents a community. The counter represents the
       ; number of vertices in this community.
       tags
10   ]

     turtles-own [
       ; Community of the vertex.
       tag
15   ]
```

Listing 4.14. *Detecting communities, step 1: definitions*

Our algorithm will need the Network extension to load a graph, and the Table extension, which provides associative tables. The latter are required for the global tags variable, which records the number of times that each label is used in the graph. We will update this table so that it only contains tags currently in use. The size of the table will therefore indicate the number of communities detected while the algorithm is running, but we will also save this value in the global components variable so that it is easier to display in the graphical interface.

We will assign a tag label value to each turtle-node.

```
     to setup
       ca
       set tags table:make
       set-default-shape turtles "circle"
5    load-graph
       ; The number of initial communities is equal to the number of vertices.
       set components count turtles
       reset-ticks
     end
```

```
     ; Load and initialize a graph.
     to load-graph
       ; Load the graph in GraphML format
       nw:load-graphml "test.graphml"
15     ; Format the graph with an algorithm based on forces.
       repeat 5000 [ layout-spring turtles links 0.2 5 1 ]
       ; Assign a unique tag/community to each turtle: its NetLogo identifier.
       ask turtles [
         set tag who
20       ; Assign a color to each tag.
         set color one-of base-colors ; there are only 14 base-colors...
         ; Save the tag.
         increment-tag tags tag
       ]
25   end
```

Listing 4.15. *Detecting communities, step 2: initialization*

We begin the algorithm by initializing the global variables and loading the graph. The load-graph method uses the Network extension to load the graph, which we already used in the previous section (section 4.6). Each turtle is assigned a unique label using the NetLogo who function, which returns the numeric identifier of each turtle. Colors are assigned randomly (unfortunately NetLogo only supports 14 base colors).

Each time that a new label is encountered, we use the increment-tag function, which is shown below together with the function that performs the reverse operation, decrement-tag:

```
     ; Increments the usage of a given community/tag, or creates it with counter
           equal to 1.
     to increment-tag [table t]
       ifelse table:has-key? table t [
         table:put table t table:get table t + 1
5      ] [
         table:put table t 1
       ]
     end

10   ; Decrements the usage of a given community/tag, or deletes it if the
           counter becomes equal to 0.
     to decrement-tag [table t]
       let tagcount table:get table t - 1
       ifelse tagcount = 0 [ table:remove table t ] [ table:put table t tagcount
           ]
     end
```

Listing 4.16. *Detecting communities, step 3: counting labels and communities*

These functions help to manage the associative table that keeps track of all labels. As stated above, this table relates each label to the number of vertices with that label; `increment-tag` increments this number, creating the label if it does not exist. `decrement-tag` does the opposite, and is called when a vertex of the graph changes its label. It decrements the label counter, and deletes the label if the counter becomes zero.

Finally, we need to implement the way that labels propagate:

```
1  ; Find the next possible configuration of communities.
   to next-communities
     ; Each turtle aims to adopt a new community/tag.
     ask turtles [
       ; Temporary table of neighboring communities/tags and their counters.
6      let counts table:make
       let countmax -1
       ; The neighboring community/tag most frequently encountered.
       let maxtag 0
       let maxcolor 0
11     ; Count the neighboring communities/tags.
       ask link-neighbors [
         increment-tag counts tag
         let tagcount table:get counts tag
         if tagcount > countmax [
16         set countmax tagcount
           set maxtag tag
           set maxcolor color
         ]
       ]
21     ; If the most frequent neighboring tag is different from ours,
       ; switch community.
       if maxtag != tag [
         decrement-tag tags tag
         increment-tag tags maxtag
26       set components table:length tags
         set tag maxtag
         set color maxcolor
       ]
     ]
31   tick
   end
```

Listing 4.17. *Detecing communities, step 4: propagating the labels*

The idea is to create one table for each turtle with all of the neighboring labels, and count them. We reuse the `increment-tag` function on an associative table local to each agent. We then identify the most common label within this table (as well as the color of the turtle with this label for display purposes), and if this differs from the current label, we update the current turtle and update the global table of labels, once again using `increment-tag` and `decrement-tag`.

We must now simply implement the graphical interface by adding a button for the `setup` method and a button for the iterative `next-communities` method discussed above. A monitor can be used to show the value of the global `communities` variable, indicating the number of labels in the graph. Our example graph is shown in Figure 4.8.

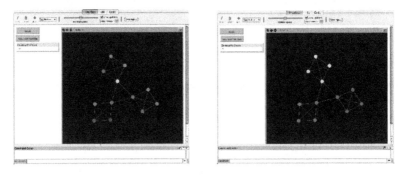

Figure 4.8. *Setting up the graphical interface to detect communities by diffusion. For a color version of the figure, see www.iste.co.uk/banos/netlogo2.zip*

5

Swarm Problem-Solving

In insect societies, the global "project" is not explicitly programmed in each individual, but emerges from the sequence of a large number of elementary interactions between individuals, and between individuals and their environment. Collective intelligence is in fact constructed from numerous simple individual elements.[1]

Jean-Louis Deneubourg

5.1. Introduction

It is increasingly common for algorithms in computer science to be inspired by "natural" models. This is not a new trend. Computer science has always drawn from its surroundings as a source of inspiration and our user interfaces are proof of this. Examples of algorithms and programming models like this include, among others, simulated annealing [KIR 83], cellular automata [VON 66], DNA computing [ADL 94, ADL 98], evolutionary algorithms [GOL 89, HOL 92] and artificial chemistry [BER 90].

Distributed programming with actor-based [HEW 73] or agent-based paradigms [FER 97, WEI 99] has reinvigorated this approach by searching for natural adaptive distributed models that can be implemented locally with

Chapter written by Antoine DUTOT and Damien OLIVIER.

1 Jean-Louis Deneubourg, "Individually, insects are stupid. Collectively, they are intelligent." *Le temps stratégique*, no. 65, Geneva, September 1995. Online text viewed on 3rd September 2014: http://www.archipress.org/ts/deneubourg.htm.

limited information. Social insects and collective movements offer a wide range of rich examples that can be used as natural metaphors for problem-solving.

In this chapter, we wish to use NetLogo to show how biological inspiration – with emphasis on collective behavioral phenomena in the animal world – can be reinterpreted in terms of modeling and programming. Specifically, we will discuss the concept of collective sorting, and in reference to section 4.2.5, the search for the shortest path in a graph as well as the dynamic aspects of these phenomena, before finally constructing solutions by exploring space with a swarm of particles.

5.2. Collective approaches

When we attempt to describe collective approaches, which involve multiple types of interaction, we often speak of collective intelligence, or swarm intelligence, which is a subcategory of distributed artificial intelligence. The term "swarm intelligence" was introduced by [BEN 93] in cellular robotics: in this context, a robot is a set of cells that self-organize depending on the task that they are processing. It was subsequently widely adopted by the computer sciences.

5.2.1. *Swarm intelligence and collective intelligence*

Swarm intelligence is inspired by the behavior of groups or societies of animals in nature. How can the individual members of a colony of ants, which seem so unsophisticated to us, construct nests that are hundreds of times larger than their builders, organized and structured so as to support the communal coexistence of a huge number of individuals, comparable to cities or even networks of cities extending over multiple kilometers, with storage spaces, nurseries, chambers, graveyards, temperature control, food supplies, classes of workers, warriors, and so on? The search for underlying mechanisms and ways of simulating them in order to benefit from them or discover new such mechanisms is a major axis of research in swarm intelligence and distributed artificial intelligence.

The models developed so far by biologists and computer scientists allow us to simulate some of the behavior of some kinds of social and eusocial animals[2]. Examples include the building behavior exhibited by termites, bees and wasps, the hunting behavior of ants and the behavior of schools of fish, flock of birds, herds and packs. These models are based on formalisms, often quite simple, which describe the behavior of individuals within a group, rather than a description of the general evolution of the group.

Collective systems are often capable of learning, adapting to change, exhibiting resilience against unexpected scenarios, etc., not at individual levels but as a group. The distinctive feature of these approaches is that the individuals that make up the swarm usually behave very simply, and in general reactively, which is of great interest for computational approaches.

Distributed models (individual-based, agent-based, based on some representation of the interactions, etc.) portray the phenomenon at a level that allows us to observe the formation of organization and the emergence of shapes within the group. They allow us to model, describe and study the interactions of individuals with other individuals and with the environment. Explicitly modeling these interactions allows us to observe several things:

– the creation of subgroups of individuals within the population;

– the construction of elements in the environment;

– the way that castes operate;

– the feedback effects exerted by these elements on these subgroups and the population.

Of course, this list is not exhaustive, however, it does indeed show that individual-based modeling provides a range of essential elements that we can adapt and exploit for other purposes.

More precisely, what do we mean by a collective approach? All collective approaches have the following definition in common: *behavior of a population of individuals that interact locally with each other and with their environment.*

---

2 Eusocial societies are characterized as follows: cooperation to care for young; absence of clear distinction between different generations, with an overlap between at least two generations; existence of individuals specializing in reproduction; division of labor, polyethism between castes or age-groups. This footnote only gives a brief idea of the notion of eusociality, in reference to [MIC 69] and Wilson [WIL 05, WIL 00]. For a wider discussion, readers can refer to [CRE 95].

This definition is naturally very general, and therefore imprecise. It reiterates the quote by Jean-Louis Deneubourg given at the beginning of this chapter, which more specifically targeted societies of insects. The quote, however, also introduces the idea of a "global project" that is not explicitly programmed in the insects' behavior, and talks about "collective intelligence", which we can define as the *"behavior of a population of individuals with simple capacities whose* local *inter-individual and environmental interactions result in the emergence and execution of a global project that is not explicitly programmed"*.

These two definitions emphasize the local nature of interindividual interactions. These models are indeed characterized by the fact that they are completely decentralized. Although many colonies of insects have what we call a "queen", these individuals, which have attracted the interest of human observers for anthropomorphic reasons, are confined to reproduction and never possess a global understanding of the state of the colony, and only ever issue orders and instructions that pertain to general behavior[3].

This last definition might seem incomplete, as it does not appear to specify how this global project will be executed. It only speaks of simple behavior at the levels of individuals, who have no global perspective and no understanding of the global project.

The answer lies in the very large number of interactions between individuals and with the environment.

5.2.2. *Interactions, self-organization and stigmergy*

In the mechanisms of swarm intelligence, we can recognize some of the elements mentioned earlier [BON 97a, BON 97b]:

– existence of multiple interactions: individual behaviors may influence and constrain each other;

– amplification by positive feedback: for example, when ants are foraging, the chemical trail of pheromones left by those that find a source of food prompts other congeners to follow the same path and reinforce it;

---

3 However, due to its unique role, the reproductive individual exerts a much stronger influence on the colony, and affects all other individuals. This is the case in all eusocial populations.

– existence of negative feedback: for example the evaporation of pheromones, which allows ants to abandon unfruitful paths;

– amplification of fluctuations: behavior is not fully deterministic, which introduces novelty and diversity by creating new positive feedback loops. This allows ants to discover and exploit new sources of food [RES 94].

In social insect colonies, interactions are therefore a fundamental component of collective dynamics. However, this usually takes the form of indirect interactions, notably by modifying the environment. The environment is in fact a medium of communication on which individual actions leave a mark (trace): this is called stigmergy. We will reuse this metaphor extensively in our computational creations.

A formal definition of stigmergy[4] is given by [KEN 01]: *mode of communication that modifies the state of the environment in such a way as to affect the behavior of others, turning the environment into a stimulus.*

In general, we can distinguish between two types of stigmergy:

1) qualitative stigmergy;

2) quantitative stigmergy.

The first type introduces the idea that semantics can be attached to the message deposited in the environment. The second introduces the concept of attraction in autocatalytic processes. In fact, most examples of quantitative stigmergy are also, of course, qualitative.

Stigmergy is part of a systemic loop; the environment (self)-organizes, structures itself by the action of the entities that exist within it, and in turn exerts an influence on these same entities.

So, stigmergy offers a distributed mechanism for controlling and coordinating that allows tasks to be executed. Self-organization is a side-effect,

---

4 We could also have chosen the definition from [GRA 59]: *"Tasks are coordinated, constructions are regulated not directly by the workers, but by these constructions themselves. 'Workers do not direct their own work; they are guided by it.' This particular kind of stimulation is what we call stigmergy (stigma: mark, ergon: work, action = stimulating action)"*.

the result of an emergent computation [FOR 91] expressed in the form of global coherence generated by local interactions.

5.3. Collective sorting

Ants have the ability to collectively sort objects. This ability has long attracted the interest of naturalists, who in particular like to observe ant "graveyards".

Figure 5.1. *Ant corpses. Source: [BIA 12]*

If corpses are placed in a petri dish, ants will group them into a heap within a few hours, as shown in the photo in Figure 5.2.

Depending on the species of ant, they can also sort brooding objects such as eggs, larvae and nymphs. In the next section, our goal will be to model this kind of collective sorting by attempting to model the behavior of ants.

5.3.1. *Ant behavior*

Ants behave in an extremely simple way. Each ant is capable of taking a larva, moving through the environment and putting it down within this environment. The rules governing this behavior are probabilistic: each ant moves randomly through its environment, and once it encounters a brooding object in a heap, the lower the density of the heap, the more likely the ant will pick up the object. Conversely, it is more likely to deposit whatever it is carrying onto a heap if the heap is dense.

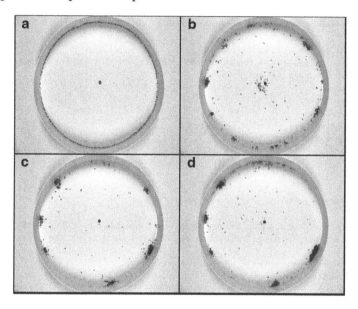

Figure 5.2. *Collective sorting. Source: [THE 02]*

Thus, patches contain the various objects in the brood: eggs, larvae and nymphs, with fixed colors. There can only be one single object on each patch. The environment is organized as a grid with patches of different colors. Black patches are unoccupied, and the others are filled with brood objects. At each time step, the turtles representing the ants randomly move to an adjacent tile. When an ant carries an individual at some stage of metamorphosis, it takes the color that represents this stage, otherwise they are arbitrarily colored white. Once an unladen ant arrives on a colored patch, it checks the number of patches with this same color in its neighborhood. If this number is low, then it has a high chance of picking up the object. It then takes on the color of the patch, which becomes black. Conversely, once an ant carrying an object with color c arrives on a patch, it counts the number of neighbors of this patch with color c. If this number is high, it will deposit its load based on a random lottery, changing the color of the patch and once again becoming white.

```netlogo
;;==================================================
;;
3 ;; We create the turtles that will become ants
;;
;;==================================================
to setup
  ca ; Clean up the world, variables...
8 initPatches ; Initialize the world with the objects/larvae to be sorted
  crt ants ; The turtles are ants!!!
  ask turtles
  [ set shape "ant"
    set size 2
13  set color white ; white ant = unladen
    setxy random-xcor random-ycor
  ]
  reset-ticks
end
18
;;==================================================
;;
;; Fix the number of objects to be sorted (numObjectsByColor for each color)
;; We will attempt to distribute them uniformly depending on the size
23 ;;
;;==================================================
to initPatches
  ask patches [
    if ( random-float (( world-width * world-height) / (numObjectsByColor *
        colors)) < 1)
28  [ set pcolor ( random colors ) * 20 + red ]
  ]
end


;;==================================================
33 ;;
;; The patches contain brood objects
;; At each time step, the ants move onto an adjacent square;
;; If an ant arrives on a colored square, it can "pick it up" or leave it
;; If the local density if its color is low, it will tend to pick it up
38 ;; Otherwise it will tend to leave it.
;;
;; If an ant is carrying a color, it can deposit it or keep it
;; If the local density of the color is high, it will tend to deposit it;
;; If it is low, it will tend to keep it.
43 ;;
;;==================================================
to brood
  ask turtles [
    ifelse hidden? [ ht ] [ st ]
48  ifelse ( color = white ) ; The ant is unladen
    [ if ( pcolor != black ) ; The patch is occupied
      [
        if count neighbors with [pcolor = [pcolor] of myself] <= random 6
          [ set color pcolor ; The ant takes the larva
```

```
53        set pcolor black ; The patch is no longer occupied
        ]
      ]
    ]
    [ if ( pcolor = black ) ; If the ant is carrying something it checks
        whether the patch is empty
58     [
        if count neighbors with [pcolor = [color] of myself] > random 6
        [
          set pcolor color ; It deposits it
          set color white ; It is unladen
63      ]
      ]
    ]
    set heading heading + random 60 - random 60
    fd 1
68  ]
    tick
  end
```

Listing 5.1. *Brood sorting*

The NetLogo (world) is configured as follows:

Location of origin	Corner, bottom left
max-pxcor	100
max-pycor	100
world wrap horizontally	☐
world wrap vertically	☐
view update	on ticks

Figure 5.3 shows different stages in the progression of the simulation. First, the initial state (Figure 5.3(a)), where the brooding objects are uniformly distributed throughout the environment, followed by the subsequent states of the brood with the emergence of order in the form of heaps (Figures 5.3(b) and 5.3(c)), and finally three heaps corresponding to eggs, nymphs and larvae (Figure 5.3(d)). The number of of elementary moves (1 patch) is 202,039,800.

5.3.2. *Model analysis*

At this point, it is interesting to discuss the nature of this model. We are considering a stigmergic process in which the environment self-organizes and develops structure by means of our virtual ants simulated by NetLogo turtles, as evidenced by the emergence of different heaps over time. These heaps in turn act upon the ants present in the virtual environment by prompting them to deposit objects on the heaps. But does this truly represent a phenomenon of collective intelligence?

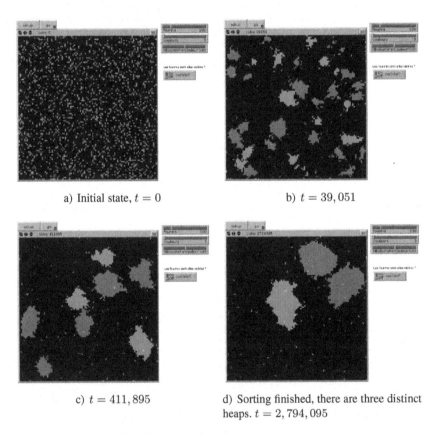

a) Initial state, $t = 0$ b) $t = 39,051$

c) $t = 411,895$ d) Sorting finished, there are three distinct heaps. $t = 2,794,095$

Figure 5.3. *Simulation of brood sorting, three stages of metamorphosis, 100 ants/turtles and 530 objects in each stage. For a color version of the figure, see www.iste.co.uk/banos/netlogo2.zip*

We can repeat these simulations with the same initial parameters but fewer ants. If we reuse the same fixed values from Figure 5.3, we observe that although the number of ants decreases, there are ultimately always three heaps, even with a single ant. This result has been confirmed and extended by simulation in [MAR 02], and a formal proof is given in [GAU 07]. We can also vary the density of the objects distributed throughout the environment, and as the authors of [DEN 91] note, we observe that there is a minimum density threshold required for heaps to emerge.

In this model, although there are positive feedback mechanisms that amplify the process by forming heaps, there are no negative feedback mechanisms to limit it. Later, in section 5.4, we will consider an example that incorporates and requires this kind of feedback to regulate the process.

In conclusion, the natural model of brood sorting has inspired a number of classification algorithms, descriptions of which can be found in [HAM 10]. The general idea is the following: the information to be sorted is arranged within a space, and the virtual ants have the ability to move them through space depending on a distance criterion that reflects the degree of similarity between objects.

5.4. From food sourcing to finding the shortest path

Jean-Louis Deneubourg *et al.* observed and demonstrated that some species of ants are capable of choosing the shortest path to reach a food source. To show this, they devised a particularly clever experiment [GOS 89, DEN 90] in the form of a double binary bridge between a food source and a nest of Argentine ants (*Linepithema humile*).

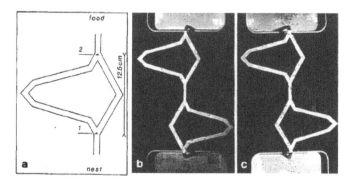

Figure 5.4. *Double binary bridge. Source: [GOS 89]*

The observed mechanism is based on a local and indirect mode of communication. Ants can deposit chemical molecules known as pheromones into the environment. These molecules are attractive and attract other ants, who are then enlisted to forage for food. This reinforces the chemical deposit; P.P. Grassé [GRA 59] writes of stigmergy, which he defines as: "stimulating workers through the actions that they perform", as we noted previously.

Ants continue to randomly explore the environment around their nest. When one or several ants find food, they bring it back to the nest, depositing pheromones along their path. These pheromones attract neighboring ants who are not yet carrying food, which follow the trail back to the food before returning to the ant colony, in turn reinforcing the pheromone trail. If multiple paths are possible, the shortest will be used by more ants, and so will be more attractive. Since pheromones are volatile, they evaporate, and in doing so penalize longer paths. Note that ants only tend to follow the paths. Each ant can leave the marked path and discover a new one. This kind of fluctuation allows ants to adapt to changes in the environment, such as the sudden apparition of an obstacle.

The ants exhibit self-organization, and four characteristics emerge [BON 99]:

1) numerous and multiple interactions;

2) fluctuations;

3) a positive feedback mechanism that creates an amplification phenomenon. A strongly marked path will attract other ants, which will reinforce it in turn;

4) a negative feedback mechanism that allows the process to be regulated. In the case of pheromones, this is evaporation.

The experiment by Deneubourg *et al.* uses a constrained space representing a network of connections, which can be modeled by a graph. It shows that Argentine ants are capable of finding the shortest path in a graph by their food-sourcing algorithm. We will use the example of this experiment to construct a bioinspired algorithm to search for the shortest path in a graph.

5.4.1. *From the natural model to the virtual model*

Consider a graph $G = (V, A, \nu)$ modeled by vertices $v \in V$ and edges given by unordered pairs of vertices $a \in A$ such that $a = (v_i, v_j) \in V \times V$. This graph is equipped with a mapping $\nu : A \to \mathbf{R}^+$.

Virtual ants roam through the graph and deposit virtual pheromones throughout the environment of the graph G in the form of numerical values attached to each edge, which determine the values of the mapping ν. Ants move through the graph according to these values, which are interpreted as probabilities. Suppose that an ant coming from the vertex O is located on the vertex A, and that from there it can travel to the vertices B, C and D via edges with 10, 30 and 20 units of pheromone (Figure 5.5(a)). It would take the edges (A, B) with probability $1/6$, (A, C) with probability $1/2$ and (A, D) with probability $2/3$ (Figure 5.5(b)). The ants construct the path on the way over between the start vertex and the end vertex, and on the way back they mark the paths by adding pheromones to the edges that they take. This implements the positive feedback mechanism.

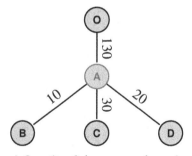
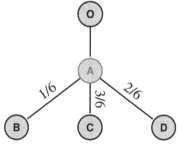

a) Quantity of pheromones, the ant is at A and can only go to B, C and D, as it already came from O.

b) Converting quantities of pheromones into probabilities. The ant is more likely to take the edge (A, C) than the edge (A, B) or the edge (A, D).

Figure 5.5. *Example of a subgraph with pheromone deposits. The ant is assumed to be located at vertex A*

Negative feedback consists of decreasing the value of the quantity of pheromone on the edges at each time step. Fluctuations are introduced by the probabilistic nature of the ants' decision-making. Modifications to a path are therefore possible, and the best path can be rediscovered once again.

5.4.1.1. *NetLogo code*

We will begin by constructing the graph for the double binary bridge. To do this, we define a specific breed of turtle, which we will call nodes. Each node knows its own identifier node-id. We define two global variables nest and food-source to store the start and finish nodes. Each edge (link) will also store the value of a quantity of pheromone, written pheromone. The positions list specifies the vertices and their positions within the NetLogo world $[[id - node_1[xy]]...[id - node_n[xy]]]$. The edges list specifies the pairs of connected vertices.

The NetLogo world is configured as follows:

Location of origin	Center
max-pxcor	30
max-pycor	30
world wrap horizontally	☐
world wrap vertically	☐
view update	on ticks

```
    globals [
      food-source ; finish node
      nest ; start node
5   ]

    breed [nodes node] ; To construct the graph
    nodes-own [node-id] ; Node identifier
    links-own [pheromone] ; Quantity of pheromone deposited on the edge
10
    ;;===============================================
    ;;
    ;; Initialization function.
    ;;
15  ;;===============================================
    to setup
      ca
      setup-graph
      reset-ticks
20  end
```

```
  ;;==================================================
  ;;
  ;; Graph creation function
25 ;;
  ;;==================================================
  to setup-graph
    let positions [[1 [0 -27]] [2 [0 -20]] [3 [27 -12]] [4 [-6 -12] ] [5 [0
        0]] [6 [10 6]] [7 [-22 6]] [8 [0 20]] [9 [0 27]]]
    let edges [[1 2] [2 3] [2 4] [3 5] [4 5] [5 6] [5 7] [6 8] [7 8] [8 9]]
30  set food-source 9
    set nest 1
    set-default-shape nodes "circle"
    foreach positions [
      create-nodes 1 [
35      set color blue
        set size 3
        set node-id first ?
        setxy first last ? last last ?
      ]
40  ]
    foreach edges [
      ask get-node first ?
      [
        create-link-with get-node last ?
45      [
          set pheromone 0.1 ; To avoid dividing by zero
          set thickness 0
        ]
      ]
50  ]
  end

  ;;==================================================
  ;;
55 ;; Establish id correspondence between graph node and turtle node
  ;;
  ;;==================================================
  to-report get-node [id]
    report one-of nodes with [node-id = id]
60 end
```

Listing 5.2. *Constructing the graph to represent the double binary bridge*

We now need to define the ants turtles. To do this, we create the corresponding space. Each ant moves from-a to-b, saves its path in the graph (itinerary), waits for waiting-period before leaving the nest and knows whether or not it is moving from the nest toward the food source, or vice versa (outward?). We therefore modify and extend the NetLogo code from listing 5.2.

```
    breed [ants ant] ; Ants looking for the path

 4  fourmis-own [
      from-a to-b ; From which vertex to which
      itinerary ; The path taken
      waiting-period ; Waiting period before leaving the nest
      outward? ; true -> nest to food source
 9  ]

    ;;===============================================
    ;;
    ;; Initialization function
14  ;;
    ;;===============================================
    to setup
      ca
      setup-graph
19    setup-ants
      reset-ticks
    end

    ;;===============================================
24  ;;
    ;; Create ants
    ;;
    ;;===============================================
    to setup-ants
29    create-ants num-ants [ ; fixed by a cursor on the interface
        set shape "ant"
        set color red
        set outward? true
        set waiting-period random num-ants
34      set from-a get-node nest ; Retrieve the corresponding node
        set to-b choose-destination ; Find the next vertex
        move-to from-a ; The ant rejoins the start node
        face to-b ; Face it towards the next node
      ]
39  end
```

Listing 5.3. *Introducing ants for the double binary bridge*

We now write a choose-destination function that determines the next node for a given ant located at a given node (from-a). This choice depends on the direction of movement. If it is moving from the food source to the nest, this is determined by the path (itinerary) that it took on the way there, otherwise it depends on the adjacent vertices and probabilities as a function of the quantity of pheromone, as stated above.

```
;;==================================================
;;
;; Determine the next destination of an ant, given the start vertex.
;;
5  ;;==================================================
   to-report choose-destination
     let id-of-a [node-id] of from-a
     ;; Did the ant reach the nest or the source?
     if id-of-a = food-source [ set outward? false] ; The ant reached the
            source and must return to the nest
10   if id-of-a = nest ; The ant is in the nest and must travel to the source
     [
        set outward? true
        set itinerary [] ; New path
     ]
15 ;; We now need to find the destination
     let where-to-go 0
     ifelse outward?
     [ ; Nest -> source, using pheromones and constructing probabilities
       let pheromone-quantity 0
20     let x from-a
       let proba []
       ask links with [end1 = x] [ ; Sum the quantity of pheromone on all
            edges incidence to a (a to another vertex)
         set pheromone-quantity pheromone-quantity + pheromone
         set proba lput (list pheromone self) proba ; Build a list of type
            ((quantity-1 (link vertex-i vertex-j)) .....
25                   (quantity-n (link vertex-k vertex-l))
                   ; Suppose that a -> b 10 ; a -> c 30 ; a -> d 20 ((10
                     (link a b) (30 (link a c) (20 (link a d))
       ]
       set proba sort-by [first ?1 <= first ?2] proba ; ((10 (link a b) (20
            (link a d) (30 (link a c))
       let probabilities []
30     let cumul 0
       foreach proba
       [
          let p first ?
          let link last ?
35        set probabilities lput (list ( (p + cumul) / pheromone-quantity)
              link) probabilities
          set cumul cumul + p
       ] ; ((10/60 (link a b) (30/60 (link a d)) ((60/60 (link a c))
       let rand-num random-float 1. ; rand-num e.g. 0.4
       set where-to-go [end2] of last first filter [first ? > rand-num]
            probabilities ; where-to-go is therefore d
40     set itinerary fput link [who] of from-a [who] of where-to-go itinerary
            ; save the edge in the ant's path
     ]
     [ ; source -> nest, unravel the path
```

```
         set where-to-go [end1] of first itinerary
         set itinerary but-first itinerary
45    ]
      report where-to-go
    end
```

Listing 5.4. *Determining the next destination*

The final step is to model the movement of the ants and the mechanisms of evaporation. When an ant reaches the food source and returns to the nest, it deposits pheromones on the traveled path and chooses a new destination. Otherwise, it moves toward its destination. Once each ant has moved, we update the quantity of pheromone.

```
   ;;===================================================
   ;;
3  ;; Advancing the simulation
   ;;
   ;;===================================================
   to go
     ask ants with [waiting-period <= ticks] ; The ants do not all leave at
         the same time
8    [
       ifelse hide-the-ants [ ht ] [ st ]
       ifelse distance to-b = 0   ; The ant arrives at a vertex
       [
         if not outward? [ ; It is currently returning to the nest,
13        ask link [who] of from-a [who] of to-b ; so it deposits pheromones
               on the edges that it crosses.
           [
             ifelse bias
             [ set pheromone (pheromone + deposit / link-length ) ]; The
                 quantity of pheromone is inversely proportional to the length
                 of the edge
             [ set pheromone (pheromone + deposit ) ]
18           set label pheromone
           ]
         ]
         set from-a to-b ; Choose new destination
         set to-b choose-destination
23       face to-b
       ]
       [ ; The ant is on an edge
         ifelse distance to-b <= 2 ; Is it close to the vertex?
         [ move-to to-b ] ; Yes, go directly to the vertex
28       [fd 1 + random-float 1 ; No, move forwards
         ]
       ]
     ]
```

```
         ask links [ set thickness 0 ]
33       if show-path [shortest-path]
         evaporation
         tick
      end

38
      ;;================================================
      ;;
      ;; Evaporation mechanism
      ;;
43    ;;================================================
      to evaporation
        ask links [
          set pheromone pheromone * (1 - (rho / 100)) ; rho is adjusted through
             the interface
        ]
48    end
```

Listing 5.5. *Handling movements*

We complete the code by adding a method to display the shortest path.

```
1  to shortest-path
      let current-node get-node nest
      let link 0
      ask links [ set thickness 0]
      while [current-node != get-node food-source]
6     [
        set link max-one-of links with [end1 = current-node] [pheromone]
        ask link [ set thickness 1]
        set current-node [end2] of link
      ]
11 end
```

Listing 5.6. *Displaying the shortest path*

Figure 5.6 shows the interface with its various parameters, for example allowing the quantity of pheromone to depend on the length of the traveled edge (bias). This technique is often used, allowing a concept of local quality to be introduced. Interested readers can experiment with using and turning off this parameter to see how it affects the process of constructing the solution, in particular its rapidity and stability. The quantity of the pheromone that can be deposited by an ant can also be configured, and so can evaporation. Similarly, we added a way of viewing the shortest path and the ant's movements. These options are accessed by elements in the interface.

Figure 5.7 shows the initial state of the simulation and its state after 193 time steps. The shortest path has indeed been found by the ants by factoring in time through movement, the positive feedback mechanism given by the ants depositing virtual pheromone and the negative feedback mechanism resulting from evaporation. In some simulations, we can observe that a false solution might be constructed at first, usually at an early point in the simulation (see Figure 5.7(c)), ultimately to be replaced by the correct solution due to the fluctuations introduced by randomness and negative feedback.

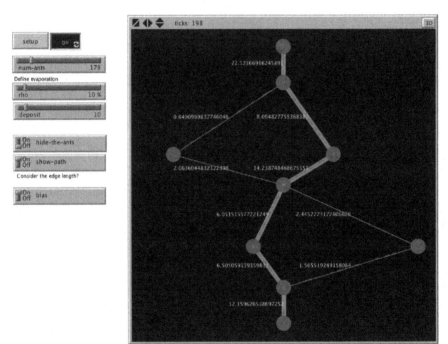

Figure 5.6. *Simulating the double binary bridge*

This characteristic can be used to introduce dynamics into the environment such as perturbations in the paths.

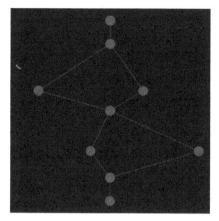

a) Initial situation. The parameters are the following: 179 ants, 10% evaporation, amount of pheromone deposited 10 units divided by the length of the edge (`bias`)

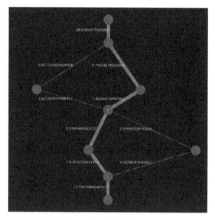

b) State after 193 time steps

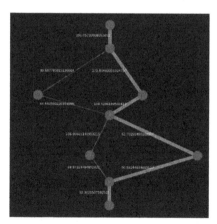

c) Incorrect solution

Figure 5.7. *Result of the double binary bridge simulation*

5.4.1.2. *Introducing perturbations*

Perturbations are introduced as a way of modifying the length of the initial paths. The code shown here mostly reuses the code given in the NetLogo model library [WIL 13].

```
;;=================================================
;;
;; Possibility to interactively modify edge size during simulation
4  ;;
;;=================================================
to modify-graph
   if mouse-down? [
      let candidate min-one-of nodes [distancexy mouse-xcor mouse-ycor]
9     if [distancexy mouse-xcor mouse-ycor] of candidate < 1 [
         let selectedants ants with [from-a = candidate or to-b = candidate]
         watch candidate ; Highlight selected vertex
         while [mouse-down?] [
            display
14          ask subject [ setxy mouse-xcor mouse-ycor ]
            ask selectedants [setxy mouse-xcor mouse-ycor face to-b] ; We cheat,
               placing the ants on
                                                          ; edges
                                                               incident
                                                               to the
                                                               vertex
                                                          ; being
                                                               moved
         ]
19       reset-perspective
         ]
      ]
   end
```

Listing 5.7. *Modifying the graph*

We update the interface (see Figure 5.6) by adding a button allowing this method to be called. We can now test the adaptive character of the algorithm by modifying the graph during simulation. To do this, we can, for example, modify the initial graph by toggling the longest paths (see Figure 5.8(a)).

The incorrect solution is then "forgotten" due to evaporation and the new path is discovered by the fluctuations. This property is very important and can be exploited in the context of dynamic graphs, as was done in [BER 06].

5.4.2. *The traveling salesman and Ant System*

The traveling salesman problem is what is known as a "toy problem", in the sense that it is not necessarily interesting in and of itself, but perfectly encapsulates a question shared by other more sophisticated versions of the problem, and that it can be used to give simple demonstrations of methods of solution such as an algorithm based on virtual ants. The statement is relatively simple:

STATEMENT 5.1.– Given a set of n towns connected by roads with known lengths, find the shortest path that passes through each town exactly once.

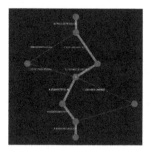

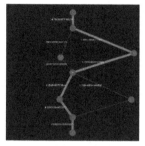
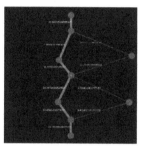

a) Graph at $t = 132$ b) Modification of graph at   c) Double binary bridge at
$t = 132$ $t = 230$ after perturbation

Figure 5.8. *Introducing a perturbation. The parameters are the following: 180 ants, 10% evaporation, quantity of pheromone deposited 10 units divided by the edge length (bias)*

There is an obvious method of solution, which is to construct all possible paths and calculate their lengths. With n towns, we will have $\frac{(n-1)!}{2}$ paths. This approach very quickly becomes intractable even for relatively low values of n, as shown by Table 5.1. With only 61 towns, there are more possible paths than atoms in the universe.

Faced with this problem of combinatorial explosion, we generally choose to turn to approximate solutions, for which we can use heuristics. There is a rich body of literature [LAP 92, REG 11] on this subject. We can classify heuristics into three categories:

1) Constructive heuristics, which gradually determine the path and add an additional time at each iteration. The stopping condition is based on finding a path. They tend to construct the best possible path.

2) Heuristics based on local searches that begin with a path and attempt to improve it by exploring the neighborhood.

3) Composite heuristics combining these two methods.

n	Number of paths	Time ($1~\mu s/chemin$)
5	12	$12~\mu s$
10	$181,440$	$0.18~s$
15	4.359×10^{10}	$12~h$
20	6.082×10^{16}	$1,928$ years
61	4.160×10^{81}	13.19×10^{67} years

Table 5.1. *Number of paths and estimated calculation time as a function of the number of vertices. The number of paths is comparable with the estimated number of atoms in the visible universe, which is 10^{80}, and the time required to enumerate all solutions is similar to the age of the universe, which is $13.798 \pm 0.037 \times 10^9$ years (data from 2014 [ADE 13])*

Algorithms based on ant colonies belong to the last of these categories, and we will present the original "Ant System" algorithm below, as proposed by Colorni, Dorigo and Maniezzo [COL 91] and show how to implement it in NetLogo.

5.4.2.1. *Ant System*

The problem is modeled by a complete graph $G = (V, A, d)$ made up of vertices $v \in V$ representing towns, and edges of unordered pairs of vertices $a \in A$ such that $a = (i, j) \in V \times V$, which represent the roads between towns. This graph is equipped with a mapping $d : A \rightarrow \mathbf{R}^+$ that specifies the distance between two towns. The Ant System (AS) algorithm uses virtual ants that deposit pheromones in the environment to mark the path that they take. In fact, this uses the same principle as in section 5.4.1, and extends the problem. We will present the initial version here, but it is worth noting that many improvements to AS have been suggested.

At first, the ants are randomly distributed over the set V of vertices. The algorithm is iterative and has two phases. In the first exploration phase of each time step, each ant chooses its next vertex. This choice depends on the distance between the vertex where the ant is located and its next vertex, and also depends on the quantity of pheromone on the edge that it can potentially choose to take (see equation [5.1]). Ants cannot return to vertices that they have already visited, which are deleted from their list of potential destinations. The second phase revolves around an updating mechanism. Once all of the ants have finished their route, the pheromones are updated based on the depositing (see equation [5.2]) and evaporation mechanisms (see equation [5.3]).

Movements are probabilistic. For an ant k located on a vertex i, the probability that it will take the edge (i, j) at time t is given by:

$$p_{ij}^k(t) = \begin{cases} \dfrac{(\tau_{ij}(t))^\alpha \times \eta_{ij}^\beta}{\sum\limits_{l \in J_i^k} (\tau_{il}(t))^\alpha \times \eta_{il}^\beta} & \text{if } j \in J_i^k \\ 0 & \text{if } j \notin J_i^k \end{cases} \qquad [5.1]$$

where J_i^k is the set of vertices visited by ant k when it is on vertex i. The quantity of pheromone on the edge (i, j) is written by τ_{ij}, and $\eta_{ij} = 1/d(i, j)$ determines the *visibility*. The α and β parameters allow the importance of pheromone trails to be calibrated relative to the visibility.

After finishing its cycle, ant k deposits a quantity $\Delta\tau_{ij}^k$ of pheromone onto the edge (i, j) (see equation [5.2]).

$$\Delta_{ij}^k = \begin{cases} \dfrac{Q}{L_k} & \text{if ant } k \text{ passed through } (i, j) \text{ during its cycle} \\ 0 & \text{otherwise.} \end{cases} \qquad [5.2]$$

L_k is the length of the cycle of ant k, and Q is a fixed parameter.

Pheromone evaporation allows suboptimal solutions to be avoided. The attraction of edge (i, j) is given by:

$$\tau_{ij}(t + n) = \rho \times \tau_{ij}(t) + \Delta\tau_{ij} \qquad [5.3]$$

$(1 - \rho)$ corresponds to evaporation, n is the order of the set V, i.e. the number of towns, and $\Delta\tau_{ij} = \sum\limits_{k=1}^{m} \Delta\tau_{ij}^k$, where m is the number of ants.

5.4.2.2. NetLogo code

We will begin by constructing the complete graph (see listing 5.8). To do this, we define a breed of turtles (`towns`), which will be connected by `links`. We also add another type of turtle to represent the virtual ants (`ants`). Each ant will be capable of remembering its past trajectory and length. An initial quantity of pheromone is also deposited on the `links`. Two global variables, `best-path` and `best-path-length`, store the best trajectory found and its length, which will be displayed in a `monitor` on the interface. The number of ants and towns is determined by a slider on the interface associated with the variables num-ants and num-towns. The full interface is shown in Figure 5.9.

The NetLogo world is configured as follows:

Location of origin	Corner, bottom left
max-pxcor	150
max-pycor	150
world wrap horizontally	☐
world wrap vertically	☐
view update	on ticks

```
    globals [ best-path best-path-length]

 3  breed [towns town ]
    breed [ants ant]

    links-own [
      tau ; Quantity of pheromone
 8  ]

    ants-own [
      where-am-i ; location of the ant (current town)
      my-path ; past trajectory of the ant
13    path-length ; length of this trajectory
    ]

    ;;==============================================
    ;;
18  ;; Initialization functions
    ;;
    ;;==============================================
    to setup
      ca
23    reset-ticks
      setup-towns
      setup-links
      create-ants num-ants
      set best-path-length 1E99 ; Choose a very large value
28  end

    to setup-towns
      set-default-shape towns "circle"
      let size 1.5
33    create-towns num-towns [
        setxy (0.5 * size-val + random-float (max-pxcor - size-val)) ; Avoid
            placing towns too close to the
```

```
         (0.5 * size-val + random-float (max-pycor - size-val)) ; edge of
              the NetLogo world
       set color blue
       set size size-val
38   ]
     end

     to setup-links
       ask towns [create-links-with other towns]
43   ask links [
       set color red
       set thickness 0.1
       set tau 1E-6 ; This quantity is introduced to avoid dividing by zero
     ]
48   end

     ;;============End initialization=================
```

Listing 5.8. *Creating a complete graph and ants*

Each ant will construct a path in the graph. If this path is better than the previously saved graph, it replaces it. We complete the NetLogo code from listing 5.8 by adding methods for this construction (see listing 5.9). This first version is only based on a random path through the towns that does not consider distances. However, we avoid going through the same town twice.

```
     ;;===============================================
     ;;
     ;; Usual go function
     ;;
5    ;;===============================================

     to go
       ask ants [
         set my-path construct-path     ; The ants construct a path
10       set path-length calcul-length my-path ; Calculate the length of the path
         if path-length < best-path-length [ ; If this is better than the
                previous best path
           set best-path-length path-length ; save it
           set best-path-length path-length
           show-best-path ; and display it
15       ]
       ]
       tick
     end

20   ;;===============================================
     ;;
     ;; Functions for constructing the path
```

```
   ;;
   ;;=============================================
25 to-report construct-path
     set where-am-i one-of towns ; Place the ant on one of the towns ;
     let path (list where-am-i) ; The path starts in the first town
     let towns-to-visit [self] of towns with [self != [where-am-i] of myself]
       ; Construct the list of towns yet to be visited
     while [not empty? towns-to-visit] [ ; While there remain towns to be
         visited
30     let where-am-i choose-new-town towns-to-visit ; Choose a new town
       set path lput where-i-go path ; Add new town to path
       set towns-to-visit remove where-i-go towns-to-visit ; Remove from list
           of towns to be visited
       set where-i-am where-i-go ; Move the ant.
     ]
35   report path
   end


   to-report choose-new-town [towns-to-visit]
40   report first towns-to-visit
   end


   to-report calcul-length [path]
45   let m but-first lput first path path ; Construct a second list m
     let length-val 0 ; path : [(town 3) (town 4) (town 0) (town 2) (town 1)]
                                       ; m : [(town 4) (town 0) (town
                                             2) (town 1) (town 3)]
     (foreach path m
       [ ask link [who] of ?1 [who] of ?2 [
50       set length-val length-val + link-length ]])
     report length-val
   end

   ;;=============================================
55 ;;
   ;; Display the best known path
   ;;
   ;;=============================================
   to show-best-path
60   ask links [
       hide-link
     ]
     let m but-first lput first best-path best-path ; Construct a second list m
     (foreach best-path m
65     [ ask link [who] of ?1 [who] of ?2 [
         set color yellow
         set hidden? false
         set thickness 0.6]])
   end
```

Listing 5.9. *Constructing a path with ants*

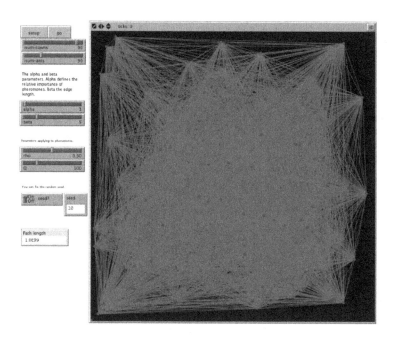

Figure 5.9. *Interface and initial state of the traveling salesman, 25 towns. For a color version of the figure, see www.iste.co.uk/banos/netlogo2.zip*

The pheromone will introduce bias into the algorithm. In the earlier version (see listing 5.9), we defined a function `choose-new-town` that returns the first town in the list of towns yet to be visited (`towns-to-visit`), which is constructed in a random order by NetLogo. We will now modify this function (see listing 5.10) in order to calculate the probability as a function of the weight of the edge and the pheromones, using equation [5.1]. The way this algorithm is written is inspired by the NetLogo code in listing 5.4. Instead of assigning the probability to the link, we assign it to the vertex incident to `where-am-i`.

```
1 to-report choose-new-town [towns-to-visit]
    let numerator 0
    let denominator 0
    let edgeweights []
    foreach towns-to-visit
6 [
      ask link [who] of where-am-i [who] of ?
      [
        set numerator tau ^ alpha * (1 / link-length) ^ beta
```

```
        set denominator denominator + numerator
11        set edgeweights fput (list numerator ?) edgeweights
      ]
    ]
    set edgeweights sort-by [first ?1 <= first ?2] edgeweights
    let p []
16  let cumul 0
    foreach edgeweights
    [
      set p lput (list ( (first ? + cumul) / denominator) last ?) p
      set cumul cumul + first ?
21  ]
    report last first filter [first ? > random-float 1.] p
  end
```

Listing 5.10. *Choosing the next town to be visited by an ant as a function of probability (see Equation 5.1)*

On the interface, we allow the user to configure α and β using the sliders associated with variables with the same names (see Figure 5.9). We also need to introduce mechanisms for positive feedback and evaporation as specified by equations [5.2] and [5.3]. This is done by the method update-pheromone which is called by the go method at the end of each cycle (see listing 5.11). The value of ρ is chosen by the user with a slider. We also make it possible to specify the random seed, so that simulations can be repeated.

```
    to setup
2     ca
      reset-ticks
      if seed?
      [ random-seed seed ]
      setup-towns
7     setup-links
      create-ants num-ants
      set best-path-length 1E99
    end

12  to go
      ask ants [
        set my-path construct-path      ; The ants construct a path
        set path-length calcul-length my-path    ; Calculate length of the path
        if path-length < best-path-length [    ; If this is better than the
            previous best path
17      set best-path my-path    ; save it
        set best-path-length path-length
        show-best-path    ; and display it
      ]
    ]
```

```
22   update-pheromone
     tick
   end


27 to update-pheromone
     ask links [ set tau (tau * (1 - rho)) ]
     ask ants [
       let m but-first lput first my-path my-path ; We construct a second list
            m
       (foreach my-path m
32        [ask link [who] of ?1 [who] of ?2 [ set tau (tau + Q / [path-length]
              of myself) ]])
     ]
   end
```

Listing 5.11. *Updating the pheromones (see equations [5.2] and [5.3])*

It is now possible to explore the influence of these parameters, and also compare this metaheuristic with others, such as simulated annealing or genetic algorithms, but we can also compare it with improvements such as the idea of introducing elitism by increasing the influence of the best path, as was done in Figures 5.10 and 5.11. The details of this improvement are left as an exercise for the reader.

5.5. The intentions of a swarm

In 1995, a sociologist, James Kennedy, and an electrical engineer, Russel C. Eberhart, explored the idea of social interactions as a computational model. Rather than focusing on advanced cognitive capacities, they examined interactions between individuals. One of their primary sources of inspiration was the way that flocks of birds form, and how they feed themselves and communicate about sources of food. They were inspired by the work of Craig Reynolds [REY 87], and Heppner and Grenander [HEP 90]. They developed an optimization model that they named "particle swarm optimization" or *PSO*, which we propose to implement in NetLogo.

As early as 1985, Craig Reynolds suggested a particularly simple model [REY 87] for imitating certain flocks of birds, which he named *boids* (bird-oids, like humanoids). This model was based on the principle that individuals only perceive their congeners within a limited neighborhood, usually within a fixed angle of vision, and that there are three rules:

1) Cohesion: individuals want to get closer to their neighbors.

2) Separation: if the distance between them is too small, individuals pull away to avoid collision.

3) Alignment: individuals imitate the average alignment of their neighbors.

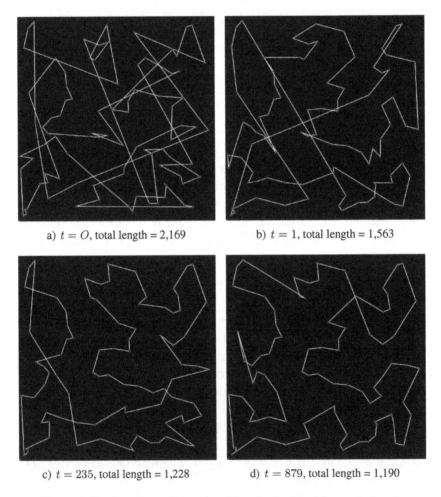

a) $t = O$, total length = 2,169   b) $t = 1$, total length = 1,563

c) $t = 235$, total length = 1,228   d) $t = 879$, total length = 1,190

Figure 5.10. *Traveling salesman problem, solved by AS.* $\alpha = 1$, $\beta = 5$, $\rho = 0.5$, *num-towns* = *num-ants* = *90*, $Q = 100$, $\tau_0 = 10^{-6}$

In general, individuals start with a certain speed, and have a certain momentum. Applying these simple rules with parameters to describe their importance and modifying other parameters that, for example, describe the angle of vision and the momentum allows a wide range of animal formations observed in nature to be reproduced, such as swarms in compact groups, columns of fish, herds of grazing animals, etc. Distinct groups can also form. This can in particular be achieved by introducing different types of boid, for example with predatory behavior.

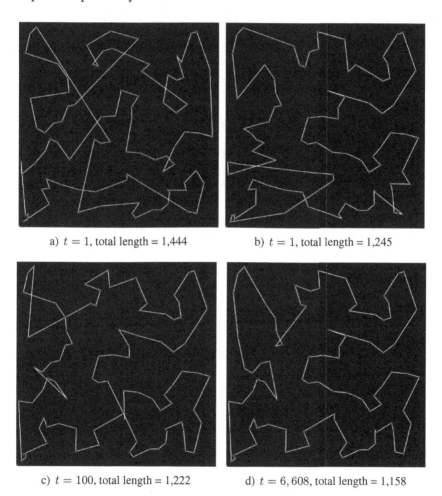

a) $t = 1$, total length = 1,444   b) $t = 1$, total length = 1,245

c) $t = 100$, total length = 1,222   d) $t = 6,608$, total length = 1,158

Figure 5.11. *Traveling salesman problem, solved by AS with elitism.*
$\alpha = 1$, $\beta = 5$, $\rho = 0.5$, *num-towns* = *num-ants* = *90*, $Q = 100$,
$\tau_0 = 10^{-6}$, $e = 5$

One of the greatest advantages of this approach, like the models we saw earlier, is that it works without global orchestration, as seems to be appropriate for the equivalent natural phenomena. The library of NetLogo models offers an implementation of this model in *Sample Models → Biology → Flocking*, as shown in Figure 5.12.

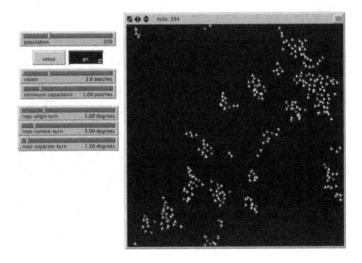

Figure 5.12. *Model of boids in the NetLogo library*

Another important aspect of this model is given by the mechanisms of interaction that it implements, such as imitation (*boids* align with their neighbors). This is also one of the driving ideas of PSO, which draws its inspiration for this from the cultural models proposed by Axelrod [AXE 97], in which individuals are informed by their neighbors of whether they are close to or match exactly with an ideal (either physically or in terms of their attributes). In these models of adaptive culture, three basic principles emerge [KEN 01]:

1) Evaluation: ability to evaluate stimuli as either positive or negative, attractive or repulsive.

2) Comparison: ability to compare oneself to others, and compare results.

3) Imitation: after evaluating one's own state, and comparing it to others, imitate it if doing so is useful.

This kind of behavior is observed in birds. If an area of a field is discovered with new shoots, more and more birds will quickly flock to that area.

These sources inspired the model proposed by Kennedy and Eberhart. Their algorithm involves large numbers of individuals that are abstracted as *particles*. These particles are placed in a space (or hyperspace, the number of dimensions can vary) representing the problem so that the positions of individuals represent a potential solution to the problem, just as the location of food sources can vary. Just like the boids, these individuals move throughout the space.

The basic idea of PSO is the following: due to a metric that describes how well adapted they are to the problem (*fitness*), they can *evaluate* the quality of their position in space. In the basic form of the algorithm, each individual knows the best values found by the others, and so can *compare* itself to others by interacting with them. If the value found by others is better, they can attempt to *imitate* by approaching it. Individuals have memory, which allows them to remember the best position encountered during their movements. The position is also characterized by a speed and a direction, which can change. Thus, the search for the best position in space is conducted *in parallel* by all individuals, who are influenced simultaneously by their own speeds, the best solution previously identified and also the best solution found by others, due to the exchange of information between individuals.

5.5.1. *Basic model*

The NetLogo library contains a model that implements PSO based on the earliest works of Kennedy and Eberhart, which we will discuss below. Due to problems faced by this model, it was subsequently modified into a version with more localized interactions, which we will explore later by adjusting our initial algorithm.

5.5.1.1. *Model*

Having considered the metaphor in its natural setting, we now return to its application to optimization by formalizing the idea slightly. In optimization, we often need to find the values of the parameters of a function to determine its optimal value according to the criteria of a given problem. These parameters, the domains in which they are defined, and their cardinality form a space (or hyperspace with one dimension for each parameter). Finding the values of parameters that optimize the value of the function is equivalent to exploring this space. A set composed of one value for each parameter corresponds to a single point within this search space, which in our case we will view as a *particle*. The position of a particle i can therefore be seen as a vector $\vec{x}_i$. Evaluating the function at this point yields a value, which we will attempt to optimize.

Slightly varying the values of this point is equivalent to moving the particle. The algorithm works step-by-step, moving each particle in turn to search for the optimal value(s) of the function. Thus, each particle is assigned a velocity $\vec{v}_i$ that is added to the position $\vec{x}_i$ to move it for the next step:

$$\vec{x}_i(t) = \vec{x}_i(t - 1) + \vec{v}_i(t)$$

Particles remember the best position found until this point, and are aware of the set of positions of other particles, and hence the best overall position. Each particle works by moving in the direction of its velocity vector, and adjusting this vector to move closer to the best position $\vec{p}_i$ found until now, as well as the best global solution $\vec{p}_g$ found until now, which act as centers of attraction. This can be formalized as follows:

$$\begin{cases} \vec{v}_i(t) = \vec{v}_i(t - 1) + \varphi_1 \left(\vec{p}_i - \vec{x}_i(t - 1) \right) + \varphi_2 \left(\vec{p}_g - \vec{x}_i(t - 1) \right) \\ \vec{x}_i(t) = \vec{x}_i(t - 1) + \vec{v}_i(t) \end{cases} \quad [5.4]$$

This formula adjusts the velocity vector $\vec{v}_i$ of the particle i in the direction of the the the points $\vec{p}_i$ and $\vec{p}_g$. The random values φ_1 and φ_2 assign either higher or lower priority to each of these points. Including the old value $\vec{v}_i(t - 1)$ introduces some inertia into the movements. Once the velocity has been updated, we apply it to the position $\vec{x}_i$ of the particle.

The velocity in this kind of system might potentially explode. To avoid this, we define a speed V_{max} and bound v_i by V_{max}.

With this model of behavior, the particles oscillate around the barycenter [5.5] of their attraction points:

$$\frac{\varphi_1 \vec{p}_i + \varphi_2 \vec{p}_g}{\varphi_1 + \varphi_2} \quad [5.5]$$

The random φ parameters change this attraction point slightly at each step, without necessarily converging to it. We can control the changes in the trajectory by means of a weighting factor for the inertia. This is implemented in the NetLogo example (other controlling techniques exist, based on contrition coefficients [CLE 02]).

5.5.1.2. *First implementation*

Based on this model, we will now describe in detail the basic NetLogo implementation available in the NetLogo model library Sample Models → Computer Science → Particle Swarm Optimization. We will not discuss how to implement the interface, which has already been done, but we will present some of its elements as required.

The implementation works in two dimensions: it creates a landscape of patches, each of which has a real value strictly between 0 and 1 except for a single patch that contains the value 1. The objective of the exercise is of course to create a swarm of particles in the form of turtles that will attempt to find this patch. As an optimization model, we can compare this landscape to evaluating a function with two arguments, the x- and y-coordinates in NetLogo, whose image is the value of the patch corresponding to these two arguments.

Figure 5.13 shows the model interface with an example landscape.

We begin with the variables that characterize the model:

```
 1  ; Optimization model by swarms of particles, reproduced
    ; from the NetLogo model library.

    patches-own
    [
 6     val ; each patch is assigned a "fitness" value. The objective of the swarm
           ; of particles is to find the patch with the best fitness value.
    ]

    turtles-own
11  [
       vx ; velocity on the x-axis.
       vy ; velocity on the y-axis.

       personal-best-val ; best value encountered until now.
16     personal-best-x ; x-coordinate of the best value.
       personal-best-y ; y-coordinate of the best value.
    ]
```

```
   globals
21 [
     global-best-x ; x-coordinate of the best value found by the swarm.
     global-best-y ; y-coordinate of the best value found by the swarm.
     global-best-val ; best value found by the swarm.
     true-best-patch ; patch containing the best value.
26 ]
```

Listing 5.12. *Initial PSO model (data structures)*

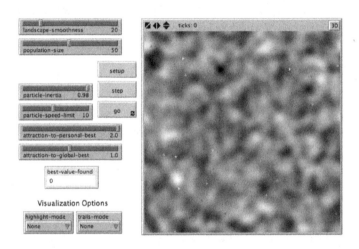

Figure 5.13. *Initial state of the model, with its landscape and default values, after calling* setup

Each patch is therefore associated with a value val, which corresponds to evaluating the objective function whose values are given by the coordinates of the patch. Each turtle is a particle, and is naturally aware of its own position. They are assigned a velocity in each dimension, vx and vy. To implement particle memory, i.e. the best position found until now, we use three variables: personal-best-x and personal-best-y, which store the best position, and personal-best-val, which stores the value at this position.

Finally, to allow particles to communicate, we use global variables to save the best position found until now, similarly to how the positions are saved by each individual particle. Each particle-turtle has access to this and can compare itself to it. Thus, in some sense, all particles are able to communicate with each other.

Although in a real problem setting we will not necessarily be able to recognize the solution value as such, this is an example, and the global variable `true-best-patch` stops the model when the best value is found.

Next, we create the patch landscape:

```
to setup-search-landscape
  ; Create a hilly landscape.
  ask patches [ set val random-float 1.0 ]

  ; Smooth the landscape.
  repeat landscape-smoothness [ diffuse val 1 ]
  let min-val min [val] of patches
  let max-val max [val] of patches

  ; Normalize the values between 0 and 1 (0.9999 to make sure that
  ; only one single patch has value 1 for later).
  ask patches [ set val 0.99999 * (val - min-val) / (max-val - min-val) ]

  ; make sure that one single patch contains the global optimum, which has
      value 1.0.
  ask max-one-of patches [val]
  [
    set val 1.0
    set true-best-patch self
  ]

  ask patches [ set pcolor scale-color gray val 0.0 1.0]
end
```

Listing 5.13. *Initial PSO model (initializing the landscape)*

The procedure assigns a random value to each patch, then uses the value of the `landscape-smoothness` interface to "smooth" the patches relative to each other by several iterations of diffusion. Finally, we normalize the values strictly between 0 and 1, and select a random patch to give it the value 1.

Thus, the initialization procedure creates this landscape, and creates a certain number of turtles (`population-size`, configurable in the interface) to model the swarm particles.

```
   to setup
     ca
3  setup-search-landscape

     ; create the particles and position them randomly.
     create-turtles population-size
     [
8      setxy random-xcor random-ycor

       ; to each particle, assign a random velocity according to a normal
           distribution
       ; centered around zero with a standard deviation of 1, in both the x-
           and y-directions.
       set vx random-normal 0 1
13     set vy random-normal 0 1

       ; the starting point is also the best known position until now.
       set personal-best-val val
       set personal-best-x xcor
18     set personal-best-y ycor

       ; choose a random NetLogo base color, excluding gray.
       set color one-of (remove-item 0 base-colors)

23     ; make the particle easier to see.
       set size 4
     ]
     update-highlight
     reset-ticks
28 end

   to update-highlight
     ifelse highlight-mode = "Best found"
     [ watch patch global-best-x global-best-y ]
33   [
       ifelse highlight-mode = "True best"
       [ watch true-best-patch ]
       [ reset-perspective ]
     ]
38 end
```

Listing 5.14. *Initial PSO model (turtle initialization)*

Each particle is randomly assigned a position and a velocity. The velocity
is between 0 and 1. Of course, the current best position is the only one
encountered so far. The update-highlight method displays the best global
patch as well as the best patch found until now.

Finally, the go function implements the actual PSO algorithm. At each stage of the algorithm, each particle performs three steps:

1) Evaluation: test whether its current position is better than the best position found until now.

2) Comparison: check the best values found by the other particles.

3) Imitation: move, attracted by the particle's best position and the best position found by other particles.

This procedure is quite long, so we will split it into these three steps.

```
   to go
2    ask turtles [
       ; should particles leave a trail?
       ifelse trails-mode = "None" [ pen-up ] [ pen-down ]

       ; 1) Evaluation: update the best position found until now by each
           particle,
7      ; if necessary.
       if val > personal-best-val
       [
         set personal-best-val val
         set personal-best-x xcor
12       set personal-best-y ycor
       ]
     ]
     ...
```

Listing 5.15. *Initial PSO model (evaluation)*

In this first part, we note the value of the current patch (which we arrived at in the previous step). If it is better than the previous best recorded position, we update it. We save both the position and its value.

```
     ...
     ; 2) Comparison: update the best global position of the swarm if
         necessary.
     ask max-one-of turtles [personal-best-val]
     [
5      if global-best-val < personal-best-val
       [
         set global-best-val personal-best-val
         set global-best-x personal-best-x
```

```
        set global-best-y personal-best-y
10    ]
    ]
    if global-best-val = [val] of true-best-patch
    [ stop ]

15  if (trails-mode != "Traces")
    [ clear-drawing ]
    ...f
```

Listing 5.16. *Initial PSO model (comparison)*

In the second part, we do the same with the best global value depending on the best particle-specific value: we ask each particle for their best value, and update the global optima. If we observe that the optimal value has been found, we terminate the simulation.

```
    ...
    ; 3) Imitation :
3   ask turtles
    [
      set vx particle-inertia * vx
      set vy particle-inertia * vy

8     ; change my velocity, "attracted" by the best personal value.
      facexy personal-best-x personal-best-y
      let dist distancexy personal-best-x personal-best-y
      set vx vx + (1 - particle-inertia) * attraction-to-personal-best *
          (random-float 1.0) * dist * dx
      set vy vy + (1 - particle-inertia) * attraction-to-personal-best *
          (random-float 1.0) * dist * dy
13
      ; change my velocity, attracted by the best global value.
      facexy global-best-x global-best-y
      set dist distancexy global-best-x global-best-y
      set vx vx + (1 - particle-inertia) * attraction-to-global-best *
          (random-float 1.0) * dist * dx
18    set vy vy + (1 - particle-inertia) * attraction-to-global-best *
          (random-float 1.0) * dist * dy

      ; speed limits are especially necessary because this environment is
      ; torus-shaped, and particles can accelerate continuously on the torus
          to unreasonable speeds.
      if (vx > particle-speed-limit) [ set vx particle-speed-limit ]
23    if (vx < 0 - particle-speed-limit) [ set vx 0 - particle-speed-limit ]
      if (vy > particle-speed-limit) [ set vy particle-speed-limit ]
      if (vy < 0 - particle-speed-limit) [ set vy 0 - particle-speed-limit ]

      ; turn in the direction of my velocity
```

```
28    facexy (xcor + vx) (ycor + vy)

      ; move forwards, by an amount determined by my velocity
      fd sqrt (vx * vx + vy * vy)

33    ]
      update-highlight
      tick
    end
```

Listing 5.17. *Initial PSO model (imitation)*

Finally, the third part uses the model for movements. The first section (lines 5 and 6) starts with the `particle-inertia` parameter from the interface, which is applied to the velocity.

Next, we find (lines 8–18) the NetLogo equivalent of equation [5.4], applied in two stages, with attraction toward the best point encountered by the particle, followed by attraction toward the best global point. The φ_1 and φ_2 parameters are specified by the values `attraction-to-personal-best` and `attraction-to-global-best` from the interface, multiplied by a random value between 0 and 1 that is recalculated at each step. The inertia parameter added to the model is also taken into account via the term (1 - `particle-inertia`).

The method used to calculate the vector in the direction of the best point encountered personally or the best global point is specific to NetLogo, and deserves some explanation: we use `facexy` to point the turtle toward each of these points. Then, we calculate the distance between the turtle and these points. Finally, we use this distance multiplied by the primitive vx or vy to obtain the components of the vectors in the direction of these points. vx and vy represent one unit along the x- or y-axis in the current direction (`facexy`) of the turtle (following a unit vector). Thus, the formulas `dist * vx` and `dist * vy` give the components of the vectors pointing toward the best point encountered by the particle and the best global point, respectively.

After this, we check (lines 20–25) that the new velocity does not exceed V_{max}, which is determined by the value of the `particle-speed-limit` interface.

Finally (lines 28–31), we adjust the orientation of the turtle by that of the velocity vector, then move it a distance equal to the length of this vector.

5.5.1.3. *Results*

After using setup to initialize the landscape and the mode, we run the algorithm with the go method. We can highlight the position of the best solution by using highlight-mode set to True best, as in Figure 5.14. Similarly, it is often helpful to turn on particle trails by setting trails-mode to Traces.

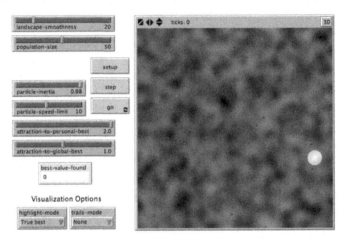

Figure 5.14. *Highlighting the target point. For a color version of the figure, see www.iste.co.uk/banos/netlogo2.zip*

When we run the model, we observe that although it does indeed find the best solution in many cases, sometimes it simply fails. The best value found is indicated by best-value-found, and is very close to 1, but sometimes the algorithm cycles around local optima instead of finding the global optimum.

Obviously, we cannot guarantee to find the optimum with this algorithm, and depending on the problem it can be difficult to know for sure that the optimum has been found, even when it has.

However, we see that over time, since all particles communicate among themselves, if they have not discovered the zone with the global optimum, then are ultimately attracted by a local optimum and bunch up around it. We can strongly influence this behavior with the inertia to force particles to follow larger cycles, but this depends on the landscape or the function with which the particles are embedded, as we can see in Figure 5.15.

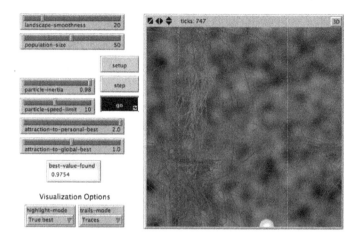

Figure 5.15. *The model is stuck inside a local optimum. For a color version of the figure, see www.iste.co.uk/banos/netlogo2.zip*

The authors of PSO very quickly identified that this behavior is linked to the fact that particles communicate globally. As we mentioned in section 5.2, interactions are almost never global in natural models. If we wish to remain true to the natural source of inspiration, the individuals in the simulation will likely communicate with their neighbors or acquaintances, but likely not with the whole group. In the cultural models mentioned earlier, knowledge is not communicated globally, but is disseminated by acquaintance.

5.5.2. *Model with local interactions*

Kennedy and Eberhart very quickly suggested a version of PSO in which the particles have a network of such acquaintances, and do not communicate globally but only within this network. In their model [EBE 95], they do not use spatial locality but locality of acquaintance, which remains invariant throughout the simulation. Usually, particles only know two, four, etc., other particles, always the same ones, and so form a network of acquaintances shaped like a ring as shown in Figure 5.16. However, other shapes are also possible.

The basic idea is that discovering a local optimum influences the network of acquaintances, and its influence diminishes over distance in the network.

Whereas with global communication individuals end up converging toward a point that might be a local optimum, networks of acquaintances allow groups to form, increasing the chance of finding the global optimum without converging to a unique point in space.

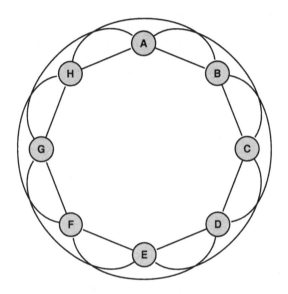

Figure 5.16. *Network of acquaintances in the shape of a ring. Each particle is connected to four others*

The notion of *link* provided by NetLogo is ideal for implementing this algorithm. We will use this mechanism, but first we should discuss how to modify the initial PSO algorithm. In the following, we will retain global search among all particles, but only for the purpose of terminating the algorithm. Apart from this, the only modification is to assign a set of "friendly" particles to each particle and program them to memorize the best value within their network of acquaintances in addition to their best personal value.

The particle motion formula remains exactly the same, except that the best global point p_g is replaced by the best point within the local network of acquaintances of the particle p_{il}.

$$\begin{cases} \vec{v}_i(t) = \vec{v}_i(t-1) + \varphi_1 \left(\vec{p}_i - \vec{x}_i(t-1)\right) + \varphi_2 \left(\vec{p}_{il} - \vec{x}_i(t-1)\right) \\ \vec{x}_i(t) = \vec{x}_i(t-1) + \vec{v}_i(t) \end{cases} \quad [5.6]$$

Let us now consider the changes that must be made to the NetLogo model above to take into account this network of acquaintances. The first change is to store the best position found within the network of acquaintances and its value, as well as the best position found individually by the particle.

```
    turtles-own
    [
4     vx ; velocity along the x-axis.
      vy ; velocity along the y-axis.

      personal-best-val ; best value encountered until now.
      personal-best-x ; x-coordinate of the best value.
9     personal-best-y ; y-coordinate of the best value.

      ; We add a variable for the best value found within the network of
          acquaintances.
      local-best-val ; best value encountered locally until now.
      local-best-x ; x-coordinate of the best local value.
14    local-best-y ; y-coordinate of the best local value.
    ]
```

Listing 5.18. *PSO model with locality (data structure)*

During initialization, we also need to create this network of acquaintances. We will use the NetLogo links to do this, with a ring-shaped network like the one described earlier. Since each particle-turtle is numbered, and since this number can be accessed with the who command, we will use it to create a link (create-link-with) with the two next particles, as if the set of particles were arranged as a torus.

```
    ; create a network of links between particles so that each particle has
    ; n neighbors (where n is even) in the form of a ring (unique, to control
        the swarm).
    to create-the-links
5     ask turtles [
        create-link-with turtle ((who + 1) mod population-size)
        create-link-with turtle ((who + 2) mod population-size)
      ]
      ask links [ set color 15 ]
10  end
```

Listing 5.19. *PSO model with locality (network of acquaintances)*

Of course, we need to slightly update the initialization method to add a call to the method for creating links (create-the-links) before update-highlight.

```
to setup
   ...
     set size 4
   ]
5  create-the-links
   update-highlight
   reset-ticks
   end
```

Listing 5.20. *PSO model with locality (Initialization)*

The method for updating particles as a function of the best personal value is expanded to include code to update the best local value within the network of acquaintances (lines 15 and after).

```
2 to go
    ask turtles [

      ...
      ; update the best position found by each particle until now
7     ; if necessary.
      if val > personal-best-val
      [
        set personal-best-val val
        set personal-best-x xcor
12      set personal-best-y ycor
      ]

      ; update the best local position found within the neighborhood
      ; if necessary.
17    let best max-one-of link-neighbors [personal-best-val]
      if [personal-best-val] of best > personal-best-val
      [
        set local-best-val [personal-best-val] of best
        set local-best-x [personal-best-x] of best
22      set local-best-y [personal-best-y] of best
      ]
```

```
      ; if local-best-val = [val] of true-best-patch
      ; [ stop ]
27    ]
      ...
```

Listing 5.21. *PSO model with locality (Local Comparison)*

Finally, the algorithm for movements is almost the same as the global version. We rename `attraction-to-global-best` to `attraction-to-local-best` in the interface. Next, instead of using `global-best-x` and `global-best-y`, we use the values `local-best-x` and `local-best-y` of the particle.

```
      ...
2     ask turtles
      [
          ...

          ; change my velocity, attracted by the best local value.
7         facexy local-best-x local-best-y
          set dist distancexy local-best-x local-best-y
          set vx vx + (1 - particle-inertia) * attraction-to-local-best *
              (random-float 1.0) * dist * dx
          set vy vy + (1 - particle-inertia) * attraction-to-local-best *
              (random-float 1.0) * dist * dy
12        ...
      ]
      ...
      end
```

Listing 5.22. *PSO model with locality (Local Imitation)*

If we run this new model, besides the fact that there are links between the particles, we see that groups form around optima distributed throughout the landscape. Thus, the models explores space better, and is likely to result in all particles converging toward a single point, as in Figure 5.17.

The article by Kennedy and Eberhart [EBE 95] studies the differences between the global and local models, and notes that the version with acquaintances tends to avoid local optima more, although it requires longer on average to find the optimum.

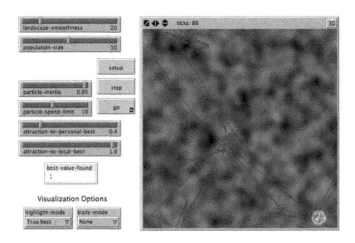

Figure 5.17. *Search with communication local to the network of acquaintances. For a color version of the figure, see www.iste.co.uk/banos/netlogo2.zip*

5.5.3. *Applications and discussion*

We now propose to apply this model to a more concrete example, although it still very much remains a "toy problem", and at the same time take the opportunity to use the GIS (Geographical Information System) extension of NetLogo mentioned in Volume 1 [BAN 15a] in section 3.6.5. To do this, we will replace the previous automatically generated landscape with data on population densities in the Île de France (Paris region), loaded with the GIS extension, and search for the most densely inhabited communes.

The data that we will use originate from the following Open Data portal:

`https://www.data.gouv.fr/fr/datasets/`

The data may be found by searching for *"données communales population Île de France"* (communal population data Île de France) [5].

They contain a "shapefile" which reproduces the limits and boundaries between the communes in the Île de France, as well as attributes specifying

---

5 `https://www.data.gouv.fr/fr/datasets/donnees-communales-sur-la-population-d-ile-de-france-idf/`.

the population densities within this communes based on various censuses. To begin with, we will show how to load these data with NetLogo, then we will replace the automatically generated landscape with these data.

5.5.3.1. *Loading the GIS data*

First, download the four data files on the page specified above, and place them in a data folder in the same place as the following NetLogo model (listing 5.23).

```
   extensions [ gis ]
   globals [ pop-dataset ]
   patches-own [ population ]

5  to setup
     clear-all
     ; Load the GIS data
     set pop-dataset gis:load-dataset
         "data/donnees-communales-sur-la-population-dile-de-france.shp"
     ; Create a link between the size of the NetLogo world and the size of the
         data.
10   gis:set-world-envelope (gis:envelope-of pop-dataset)
     ; Initialize the display.
     display-coms
   end
```

Listing 5.23. *Loading GIS data*

In this part of the model, after declaring the gis extension which is included by default in standard installations of NetLogo, we will declare a global pop-dataset variable that contains the set of downloaded geographical data. We will associate each patch with a population density value, and finally we will load the data with a setup procedure.

In order to ensure that there are sufficiently many patches, we adjust max-pxcor and max-pycor to 100 in the graphical interface. The values of min-pxcor and min-pycor will automatically be set to -100. We also set the Patch size to 4. This results in a set of 200×200 patches. Finally, we create a button for the setup method.

This method uses the gis:load-dataset command and stores the set of data read from the downloaded files, which is passed as an argument, in pop-dataset. The next command gis:set-world-envelope links the space of geographical data with the NetLogo space. It then calls the display-coms method, which is given in listing 5.24.

```
   to display-coms
 2   gis:set-drawing-color black
     ; Draw the GIS data
     gis:draw pop-dataset 1

     ; Store the data of the intersected polygon in each patch.
 7   gis:apply-coverage pop-dataset "PSDC1990" population

     ask patches [
       ; Convert the data strings into numbers, carefully avoiding
       ; NaN values for zones outside the dataset.
12     ifelse (is-string? population) [ set population read-from-string
           population ] [ set population 0 ]
       ; Color the patch as a function of the population
       set pcolor scale-color red population 200000 0
     ]
   end
```

Listing 5.24. *Displaying GIS data*

This procedure performs two actions:

1) Display the GIS data in a separate drawing layer.

2) Update the patches with the densities within each commune and assign a color accordingly.

The first action is performed by the gis-draw pop-dataset 1 command.

The second action is performed in two steps. First, the data from the GIS attributes are assigned to the population value associated with each patch. Here, we chose to use the census from 1990. The apply-coverage command uses the value of the commune that covers the largest proportion of a patch to determine which value should be assigned.

Next, for each patch, we convert this value into a color. Since some patches do not cover any commune and so do not have a value (or more precisely, have the value NaN, Not a Number), we check that the value is indeed a datastring. If so, we convert into a number, otherwise we record 0. We use scale-color between the maximum and minimum popultion to assign a scale from white to red on the patches to represent density.

Figure 5.18 shows the results.

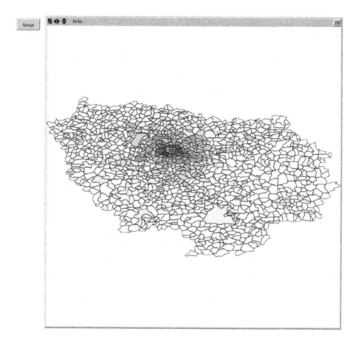

Figure 5.18. *Displaying GIS data and population density on each patch for the communes of Île de France. For a color version of the figure, see www.iste.co.uk/banos/netlogo2.zip*

5.5.3.2. *Using PSO with GIS data*

We are almost ready to reuse the earlier PSO model and apply it to the data. The first modification will be to add a population variable representing the densities on each patch.

```
patches-own [
  population ; Each patch contains a value for the population density of
        the commune where it is located.
  val ; Fitness value for PSO.
4 ]
```

Listing 5.25. *PSO with GIS data (data structure)*

The data is loaded as shown earlier.

```
1 to load-gis-data
   ; Load the GIS data.
   set pop-dataset gis:load-dataset
       "data/donnees-communales-sur-la-population-dile-de-france.shp"
   ; Create a link between the size of the NetLogo world and the size of the
       data.
   gis:set-world-envelope (gis:envelope-of pop-dataset)
6 end
```

Listing 5.26. *PSO with GIS data (loading GIS data)*

Finally, we modify the `setup-search-landscape` method by reusing the code from earlier (listing 5.27).

```
  to setup-search-landscape
    load-gis-data

4   gis:set-drawing-color grey
    ; Draw the GIS data
    gis:draw pop-dataset 1
    ; Store the data of the intersected polygon in each patch.
    gis:apply-coverage pop-dataset "PSDC1990" population
9
    ask patches [
      ; Convert the data strings into numbers, carefully avoiding
      ; NaN for zones outside the dataset.
      ifelse (is-string? population) [ set population min (list
          read-from-string population 200000) ] [ set population 0 ]
14    ; Color the patch as a function of the population
      set pcolor scale-color red population 200000 0
      set val population / 200000
    ]
    end
```

Listing 5.27. *PSO on the GIS data (Creating the landscape)*

Here, the population is normalized between 0 and 1, to fit our algorithm.

Finally, now our algorithm does not know the maximum population value, so we will allow it to keep running, and we can remove the section of code that terminates it in the go function (listing 5.28).

```
; if global-best-val = [val] of true-best-patch
2 ; [ stop ]
```

Listing 5.28. *PSO with GIS data (Model Termination)*

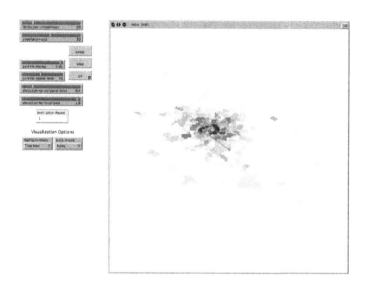

Figure 5.19. *Search for the most densely inhabited commune. For a color version of the figure, see www.iste.co.uk/banos/netlogo2.zip*

5.6. Conclusion

Throughout this chapter, we showed how some problems can be resolved by using models biologically inspired by the collective behavior observed in the animal world. These models are powerful due to their adaptability and robustness, which explains why they have permeated research fields that use descriptions phrased in terms of a large number of interacting individuals operating in a decentralized manner within a dynamic environment. This touches upon the notion of complex systems, and if we wish to study the phenomenological aspects associated with swarm intelligence by unraveling these concepts to their roots, we need to examine the concept of organization. These individuals can be observed and act as an integral part of the system to which they belong. Their actions produce feedback which in turn generates boundaries or shapes, forming organization, and at the same time developing a notion of what it means to be a part of this organization, and therefore a selection criterion. Organization thus creates interrelational connections between individuals, who become parts of a whole. It gives solidarity and robustness to these connections, and endows the system with a chance of surviving perturbations. Organization transforms, creates, connects and preserves. In [MOR 77], Edgard Morin invented the word "organisaction" to emphasize its active nature. The organization present in this type of model is derived from the system itself, and exhibits self-organizing properties that reflect the system's ability to "create itself" or "self-assemble" by producing its own, uninterrupted principles of organisaction. This self-organization is what we wish to replicate in our models, and represents the "emergent" result of calculations in the form of structures such as paths.

6

Exploring Complex Models in NetLogo

6.1. Introduction

Models and their simulators are becoming increasingly complex. They are typically the fruit of studying a phenomenon, which leads to a careful arrangement of theories, hypotheses, field data and paradigms (ODEs, PDEs, MASes, cellular automata, etc.). But the challenges and ambitions of modelers are constantly changing and in particular expanding, causing models and simulations to become increasingly expensive, both in terms of their design and analysis. Developing high-performance calculation systems and software for systematic exploration can help to iron out some of these difficulties. But, it is not enough.

Using simulation to study a model requires a large number of executions to obtain the desired results in various forms (tables, graphs and databases), which is a crucial step in evaluating, validating and developing new knowledge about the studied phenomenon. It is often impossible to conduct a comprehensive study within a reasonable time frame, given the number and nature of the parameters that need to be explored. Having to resort to innovative algorithms to reduce the domain of the parameters to be explored is unavoidable.

Chapter written by Philippe CAILLOU, Sébastien REY COYREHOURQ, Nicolas MARILLEAU and Arnaud BANOS.

This chapter aims to show how complex models may be explored by using new, distributed exploration software that makes high-performance computing resources and the corresponding exploration methods available to everyone.

6.2. Complex models and simulators

According to [TRE 08] *et al.*, a simulator is a "computer program capable of interpreting dynamic models. It is used to generate the desired perturbations" within its models. To achieve this, it uses a programming language to implement models, and routines to execute, visualize and configure them.

If we view the simulator as an instrument that breathes life into one or several models, then it also becomes a tool for manipulating these models, or in many disciplines, comes to represent the actual model itself. These kinds of simulators can be viewed as a box equipped with inputs and outputs. Their internal workings are sufficiently well understood to be recognizable, but our knowledge of the simulator-model is rarely absolute.

Simulators of complex models are inherently complex systems: they relate entities and processes via feedback loops that express themselves continuously as the model unfolds. At this point, it becomes impossible to determine the direct relationship between inputs and outputs. In order to create a response mapping for validating, calibrating and operating the model, we must first explore the parameter space. Exhaustive exploration will provide a comprehensive response mapping, but will be costly or inaccessible. Partial exploration of the parameter space produces an imperfect response mapping, but reduces the costs. Suitably adapted exploration algorithms will improve the process of producing these mappings, while simultaneously minimizing the costs associated with production.

6.2.1. *Characteristics of complex simulators*

Complex simulators are characterized by their complex internal dynamics, which are often stochastic, and their execution times, which are often long, but above all else by the way that they directly relate to the line of scientific questioning at hand.

Complex simulators are described by:

– *Strong nonlinearity*: the behavior and responses of models of dynamic systems are not deterministic, and are influenced by the presence of nonlinear relationships and feedback loops.

– *Indefinite or infinite number of reachable states*: the complex internal dynamics of these models, combined with simulation paradigms and tools, builds randomness into the results. For example, in multiagent modeling/simulation, randomness is used as an artifact to reorganize agent scheduling and to simulate a situation in which they are executed in parallel. In experimental conditions, to obtain significant behavior, we need to execute the same code a large number of times.

– *Large number of parameters to consider*: the large number of parameters combined with the simulation time and dimensions of the complex phenomenon being studied makes exhaustive exploration of the parameter space expensive or impossible. This means that deterministic methods that guarantee the global optimum cannot calculate the solution within a reasonable time frame.

– *Sensitivity of the response to the inputs*: small changes in the values of the parameters produce strong variations in the simulation outputs. This means that there are a large number of local optima, and search methods that successively iterate over the immediate neighborhood can prove ineffective.

– *Knowledge of available experimental data is often scarce*: the lack of data can make calibrating the model difficult in situations where it would be desirable to compare simulated results with real results.

6.2.2. *Inverse problem-solving by exploration: a necessity*

As stated above, complex simulators have several components: a simulation model; inputs with the measured variables and input parameters; and outputs with observable variables. This section analyzes the role of each of these components.

If we consider combinatorial optimization problems such as the *Traveling Salesman Problem* (TSP) or *Knapsack*, the number of combinations to be evaluated very quickly becomes problematic as the number of objects in the problem definition increases, assuming that an exact optimal solution is desired. If we take the more fun example of *combinatorial game theory*, the number of legal combinations on a 19 by 19 board in the Chinese game of Go was estimated to be 2.0816819938210^{170} by [TRO 07]. Even though Tromp verified this estimate in 2016 on his website, the questions raised by this game continue to challenge the best artificial intelligence programs [BOU 01] even despite spectacular progress in the last few years, most notably by the application of heuristics that are more effective than conventional approaches. In the case of discretized continuous problems, such as search for the best parameter values of a simulation, implementing a comprehensive experimental protocol (other more targeted strategies exist) poses two problems.

First, discretization does not help to solve the combinatorial problem. To give a more concrete example, if a simulation has 5 parameters, and each of these parameters are discretized into 10 steps, then there are already 10^5 possible combinations to evaluate. If we assume that the simulation model thus executed is stochastic (10 iterations), and can be run relatively quickly (1 min), then the total execution time of this procedure, despite only providing a relatively "coarse" coverage of the parameter space, is approximately equal to 2 years of calculations. Parallelizing such a calculation, i.e. executing it on multiple processors or computers in parallel, could obviously reduce this calculation time to more reasonable scales, but this does not solve a second, more restrictive problem.

If we choose this grid to discretize the parameters, we risk missing out on potential solutions. This becomes increasingly difficult and complex as the number of parameters increases, according to the phenomenon of the *curse of dimensionality* described by Richard Bellman. This problem is mainly statistical in nature; although in one case 100 points might be sufficient to begin to make inferences in a $(0..1)$ space in 1 dimension (distance of 0.01 between points), 100 points in the same $(0..1)$ space in 10 dimensions would only cover a tiny fraction of the available volume. Each point would be surrounded by a large empty region of space. Making inferences based on such a low coverage of space is unsafe. To obtain equivalent coverage, with a distance of 0.01 between each point, we would need 10^{20} points, which seems impressively high [BEL 61]. The effects of this phenomenon are visualized slightly more clearly in Figure 6.1.

Among the many tools that are available to researchers for tackling this exploratory problem, we have decided to present in this chapter a class of algorithms (evolutionary algorithms, EA) belonging to the family of metaheuristics. These probabilistic algorithms are capable of exploring large parameter spaces section-by-section without being limited by the number of dimensions. Even though these algorithms do not guarantee uniqueness or optimality of the solution (we will work in terms of local or global optima) after completing their exploration, they are superior to conventional deterministic and exact approaches in every way. Due to the two issues mentioned above (combinatorial explosion and curse of dimensionality), it would be impossible for an exact deterministic algorithm to guarantee in advance that an optimal solution will be found. To guide this exploration as best as possible, probabilistic (Es) and deterministic (for example, A*) approaches that allow suboptimal solutions can implement heuristics. The best illustration of how an algorithm based on a heuristic differs from a classical algorithm was given by [MCC 04]:

> *Here's an algorithm for driving to someone's house: take Highway 167 south to Puyallup. Take the South Hill Mall exit and drive 4.5 miles up the hill. Turn right at the light by the grocery store, and then take the first left. Turn into the driveway of the large tan house on the left, at 714 North Cedar.*

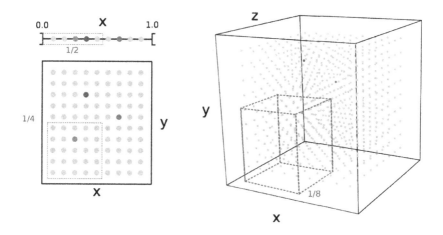

Figure 6.1. *Illustration of the effects of the curse of dimensionality on an experimental setup with 3 points strictly between 0 and 1. For a color version of the figure, see www.iste.co.uk/banos/netlogo2.zip*

Here's an heuristic for getting to someone's house: find the last letter we mailed you. Drive to the town in the return address. When you get to town, ask someone where our house is. Everyone knows us – someone will be glad to help you. If you can't find anyone, call us from a public phone, and we'll come get you.

This metaphor also illustrates the extent to which the definition of the heuristic itself can cause the algorithm to explore very different paths. In this sense, there cannot exist a perfect heuristic, only heuristics that provide better or worse results in the context of a given problem.

Using these algorithms remains expensive in terms of computation time, as a great many simulations (often several hundreds of thousands [SCH 15]) must be performed to advance the exploration procedure implemented by these algorithms. These approaches usually become impossible to implement on conventional computers as soon as the simulations begin to take longer than 1 min to run. If we wish to respect good principles of model building by viewing exploration as a systematic action that generates and measures the model dynamics each time that the modelers implement a variation in the hypotheses within the model, it is imperative that these exploration algorithms produce their results as quickly as possible. These algorithms therefore necessarily require intensive resources (high-performance computing, HPC).

6.2.3. HPC in simulations

Models and simulators are able to reproduce increasingly broad and complex phenomena at ever higher levels of expected accuracy. The resources required to execute simulations are growing, and the required number of executions is on the rise, meaning that simulation activity occupies an ever-increasing role in the modeling/simulation process.

Moreover, a vast range of computational resources are available today on networks (grid computing and clusters) and our own personal computers (CPUs and GPUs). These resources are often underutilized despite their significant potential: for example, cleverly utilizing the GPU (available in every computer) can increase the performance (in terms of memory and calculation time) by a factor of 10, 100 or even more as compared to running the same simulation agent on one single core [GIB 15]. The usage of these resources, however, remains restricted due to their very specific technical nature.

Thus, given the multidisciplinary nature of the modeling/simulation activity, and the expense involved in comprehensively studying a simulation model, designing and developing computing tools have become the most recent challenges. Finding an answer to these scientific obstacles would circumvent most of the prerequisites of HPC. This is precisely the objective pursued by a few cross-disciplinary research projects on distributed systems based on OpenMOLE and distributed algorithms specific to the world of agent-based simulation.

The topic of distributing the execution of a simulator is approached from two different perspectives in the literature: (i) distributing a simulation over multiple cores and (ii) distributing the experimental protocol over a set of cores (each simulation runs on one single core).

We will focus on the second of these points below. Readers may, however, refer to [ROU 16] for more information on distributing simulations.

Softwares, such as OpenMole, are now available that allow us to exploit these kind of resources and explore new models and algorithms.

The set of components presented in this chapter (modified model, exploration, results and graphs) may be downloaded from the following online repository: https://github.com/Spatial-ABM-with-Netlogo/Chapitre-F.

OpenMOLE is required in order to execute the exploration workflows described in this chapter (replications and calibration). A stable version is available at http://www.openmole.org/, and the most recent version is available at http://next.openmole.org/.

6.2.4. *The underlying model: NetLogo Ants*

The *Ants* simulation model by Wilensky [WIL 97] reproduces in NetLogo a model that was originally developed in StarLogo. It is available from the NetLogo website, and is included by default in the software model library.

This NetLogo model represents a colony of ants as they forage for food. Each ant follows a set of simple rules, but viewed as a whole the colony reacts in complex ways. When an ant finds a piece of food, it brings it back to its nest, and leaves a chemical trail behind it. If other ants "smell" this trail, they follow it until they reach the food. As increasingly many ants transport the food back to the nest, they reinforce the chemical trail.

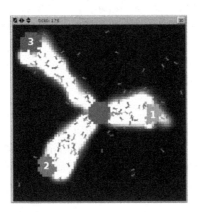

This model consists of three parameters:

– a *Population* of initial ants;

– an *Evaporation-rate* that controls the evaporation of the chemical trail;

– a *Diffusion-rate* that controls the diffusion of the chemical trail.

6.2.5. *Calibrating a model by optimization*

One conceivable way of calibrating a simulation model is to reduce it to an optimization problem. In other words, once an expert has specified criteria (data series, patterns or schematic facts [GRI 05]) for the outputs of simulation, the objective is to experiment with the model in order to test its ability to reproduce (or not) these criteria when its exploration is guided by an optimizer (which is assumed to be more sophisticated than a random walk) that ranges over a broad spectrum of admissible dynamics (initial conditions, game parameters and parameter values, mechanisms, bounds for admissible values and stopping conditions).

Whatever the output of this optimization, alone it cannot provide sufficient evidence to definitively validate or reject the assumptions embodied by the model in the context of an attempt to elucidate a complex phenomenon, since simulations are reconstructions of reality within an artificial environment (and are therefore are projections of expert knowledge that is necessarily biased and incomplete) [BUL 05] and also because the principle of equifinality in complex systems (i.e. the possibility that a system may reach the same end state by means of different initial states and trajectories) prevents us from drawing any such conclusions [REY 15].

Without going into the full details of the conventional mathematical notation typically found in this area of the literature (see [WEI 11] and [REY 15] to find out more), at least two spaces must be defined to describe how evolutionary algorithms work, which in our case will fulfill the role of optimizer.

For [WEI 11, WEI 22], the mathematical meaning of optimization is " *[...] is the process of solving an optimization problem, i. e. finding suitable solutions for it.* Optimization problems require finding *[...] an input value x^* for which a mathematical function f takes on the smallest possible value (while usually obeying to some restrictions on the possible values of x^*)*", where in this case the mathematical notation * denotes an optimal value.

The *problem space* $\mathbb{X}$ of an optimization problem may be defined as the vector containing all elements x that could be solutions. A *candidate solution* x is defined as an element of the problem space $\mathbb{X}$ of an optimization problem.

The objective of optimization is to use a suitable optimization algorithm to determine the vector of candidate solutions x^* that best fulfills the criteria defined by the user. This assumes that we are able to characterize a candidate solution x_1 in $\mathbb{X}$ relative to another candidate solution x_2 in $\mathbb{X}$.

As already discussed above, the optimizer algorithm that explores the space intelligently is guided by a heuristic function, or more precisely an objective function: *an objective function $f : \mathbb{X} \to \mathbb{R}$ is a mathematical function which is subject to optimization.*

When this objective function takes a candidate element x from the problem space $\mathbb{X}$ as a parameter, it returns a value $f(x)$ that describes its quality with respect to the optimization problem.

However, most problems will require multiple criteria to be optimized simultaneously. We will therefore directly consider the question of how to define this kind of problem, which can be summarized as follows: $min(f_1(x), \ldots, f_k(x)$ with $k > 2$.

The literature also often refers to this kind of problem by using the notation of vector functions $\vec{f}$. We define a set $\vec{f} : \mathbb{X} \to \mathbb{R}^n$ made up of n objective functions $f_i : \mathbb{X} \to \mathbb{R}$ with $\forall i \in 1 \ldots n$. Applied to a candidate solution $x \in \mathbb{X}$, this function returns a real vector of dimension n that can be projected in a space $\mathbb{R}^n$, which is also known as the *objective space* $\mathbb{Y}$.

In summary, each pair composed of one target function vector $\vec{f}$ and one candidate solution x is evaluated to give a real vector of dimension n that situates the candidate solution within the *objective space $\mathbb{R}^n$, also called* $\mathbb{Y}$.

The optimizer will choose the next candidate solution x to evaluate based on the position of the current candidate solution within this space $\mathbb{Y}$. Before discussing in any more detail the principles used by the optimizer to concretely make this decision in a multiple-criteria space $\mathbb{Y}$ that requires a compromise, we will define the problem space, the objective space and the objective functions within the context of the Ants model.

6.2.6. *Formulating objectives for the Ants model*

In the *Ants* model, we saw that there are three parameters that can be varied as model inputs.

The evaporation parameters $Evaporation - rate$ and $Diffusion - rate$ each range over the domain $\mathbb{R}$ between the values of 0.0 and 99.0. We will also define three objective functions $\{f_1, f_2, f_3\}$.

The population parameter is set to 125 ants in the colony by default, but we can also choose values in $\mathbb{N}$ between 0 and 250:

– the space $\mathbb{X}$ is a cube $\{\mathbb{N}, \mathbb{R}, \mathbb{R}\}$ bounded by $\{[0, 250], [0, 99.0], [0, 99.0]\}$;

– the space $\mathbb{Y}$ relates each point $x \in \mathbb{X}$ to a point with value f_1, f_2, f_3 in the unbounded domain $\{\mathbb{R}, \mathbb{R}, \mathbb{R}\}$.

Each of the objective functions $\{f_1, f_2, f_3\}$ are based on the time elapsed between the beginning of the simulation t_0 and the moment at which a heap of food fully disappears.

– f_1 records the time in the simulation (*ticks*) at which food heap 1 disappears;

– f_2 records the time in the simulation (*ticks*) at which food heap 2 disappears;

– f_3 records the time in the simulation (*ticks*) at which food heap 3 disappears.

The NetLogo function that computes the objective functions is given in listing 6.1. This calculation is performed at each iteration of the simulation, during the go loop.

```
  to compute-fitness
    if ((sum [food] of patches with [food-source-number = 1] = 0) and
       (final-ticks-food1 = 0)) [
3     set final-ticks-food1 ticks ]
    if ((sum [food] of patches with [food-source-number = 2] = 0) and
       (final-ticks-food2 = 0)) [
    set final-ticks-food2 ticks ]
    if ((sum [food] of patches with [food-source-number = 3] = 0) and
       (final-ticks-food3 = 0)) [
    set final-ticks-food3 ticks ]
8 end
```

Listing 6.1. *Function to calculate the objective functions*

6.2.7. *Adapting the NetLogo Ants model to be used by an optimizer*

To feed these values into the optimizer, the simulation needs to terminate somehow. We must therefore choose a *stopping condition* to substitute for a manual click on the stop button by the NetLogo user. The simplest stopping condition in this case would be to terminate the simulation when there is no longer any food available, as shown in listing 6.2. The user does not intervene, and the optimizer itself calls the function run-to-grid to execute the simulation until the stopping condition is reached.

```
   to-report go-stop?
2    ifelse (count-food > 0)[
       report true
     ][
       report false
     ]
7  end

   to-report count-food
     report sum [food] of patches
   end
12
   to run-to-grid
     setup-ants
     while [go-stop? = true ]
       [go
17     ]
   end
```

Listing 6.2. *Stopping condition for the simulation*

However, we must be careful to note that, as the optimizer attempts to find the best set of parameters values to minimize the three objective functions, it might produce combinations that push the model or model hypotheses to their limits.

For example, what happens in our simulation model if we choose the following parameter values?

We can fix the value of the random seed in the setup code in listing 6.3 to see how our program behaves. The results of this experiment are shown in Table 6.1.

```
   to setup
2    clear-all
     random-seed 42
     initialize-globals
     setup-ants
   end
```

Listing 6.3. *Choosing a random seed of 42 in the setup*

	$Population$	$Evaporation - Rate$	$Diffusion - Rate$	t_{stop}
1	125	25.0	25.0	2583 $ticks$
2	0	25.0	25.0	∞
3	25	25.0	25.0	8825 $ticks$
4	125	0.0	0.0	1374 $ticks$
5	125	99.0	0.0	1261 $ticks$
6	125	0.0	99.0	1201 $ticks$
7	125	99.0	99.0	1254 $ticks$

Table 6.1. *Let us test each of these conditions with the same random seed (42)*

– In case (2), the simulation never terminates, as the stopping condition is never met. This behavior is clearly undesirable and risks obstructing the exploration conducted by the metaheuristic. We must therefore specify a value > 0 for the ant population.

– Case (3) shows that with fewer ants, the simulation requires much longer to fulfill the stopping condition. There may therefore be very high variability in the execution times of the model, depending on the parameter values selected for its evaluation.

– Cases (4,5,6) are interesting, as they produce results that are likely counter-intuitive. Indeed, in terms of the total execution time, this random seed yields better results than randomly chosen parameter values (1).

– Indeed, in case (1), we see that poor calibration results in a vacuum effect. The ants that could potentially head toward the pile of food are diverted from their tracks by an olfactory trail that mistakenly redirects them toward the anthill.

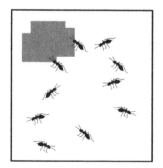 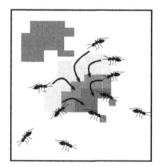

This can also be explained by a flaw in the mechanisms originally designed by the modeler, as ants cannot detect chemical trails between 0.05 and 2. However, diffusion and evaporation begin cumulating at a unit value of 60, which is equivalent to the chemical trace deposited on each patch by an ant that has found food. Therefore, in all of these cases, the model mechanisms are almost ineffective, and reduce to case (4) in which the ants simply move according to a random walk.

Will the optimizer be able to find better values in this activation zone?

If not, we will need to review either the parameters or the mechanism governing the depositing and trace detection behavior of each ant.

There are several approaches that modelers can take to avoid or limit the occurrence of behavior that might obstruct exploration:

– fixing the values of parameters that could potentially cause problems, optionally allowing them to vary at a later point;

– identifying beforehand combinations of parameter values that might cause problems, and then forbidding the optimizer from choosing them;

– introducing an artificial parameter or mechanism (in other words, one that is external to the original assumptions) into the model, for example by setting a maximum threshold of objects (turtles in NetLogo);

– introducing more restrictive stopping criteria;

– directly penalizing undesirable behavior in the objective functions.

Intensive exploration of the search space by the optimizer and the large number of executions of the simulation that this requires place great strain on the simulation process. A number of errors often resurface: division by zero, unexpected behavior, memory overflow, etc. In this sense, this kind of exploration is part of the "internal validation" of the model [AMB 06].

6.2.8. *Choosing an optimizer, evolutionary algorithms*

One of the EAs that might help us with this kind of calibration is natively included in OpenMOLE: the genetic algorithm called NSGA 2 [DEB 00].

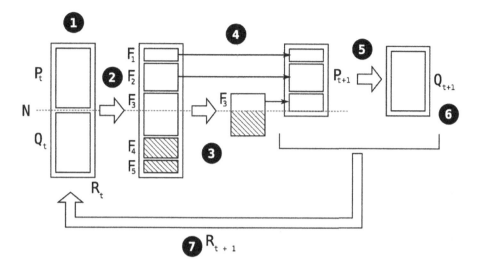

Figure 6.2. *NSGA 2 step-by-step procedure, inspired by the original diagram from [DEB 00]*

The NSGA-2 algorithm uses a population of size $2 * N$, represented in this diagram by the population R_t. In this algorithm, the best individual is guaranteed to be retained in the population R_t used to evaluate the *fitness*. This property is called *elitism* in the literature on EAs.

Due to this behavior, the first iteration I_0 of the NSGA 2 algorithm is different from the rest of the procedure, and begins with a population $P = 2*N$ of individuals with randomly initialized parameter values.

In Figure 6.2, we explain some of the most important parts of this algorithm, starting with the I_1 step:

– In step 2, the population R_t is classified using the *non-dominated sorted (NDS) algorithm* developed by Goldberg [GOL 89]. but which was only implemented for the first time in NSGA by Deb [DEB 00]. This algorithm groups individuals into successive fronts $F_{1..n}$ using a *fitness* value calculated according to the principle of Pareto dominance.

The definition of Pareto dominance and a detailed example of how to calculate it will be given at a later point in this section.

– In step 3, we see that the NSGA 2 algorithm only fully retains the fronts F_1 and F_2. The algorithm truncates the last front F_3, since the sum of the individuals from the fronts selected between F_1 and F_3 must be ultimately be equal to N.

– In step 4, the algorithm truncates F_3. But since the individuals in F_3 cannot be discriminated on the sole basis of their objective values (recall that the *fitness* values are equal for all individuals in a given front), NSGA 2 uses a specific classification based on a so-called *crowding* distance to ensure that some diversity is preserved by this truncation.

– In step 5, the offspring population Q_{t+1} of size N is generated by selecting (*binary tournament selection* based on this same crowding operator), recombining and mutating the individuals randomly selected from the population P_{t+1}.

– In step 6, this new *offspring* population Q_{t+1} is evaluated. Each individual is assigned a new vector of values obtained by evaluating this individual on each objective function.

– In step 7, the new population Q_{t+1} and the existing population P_{t+1} are merged into the population R_{t+1}.

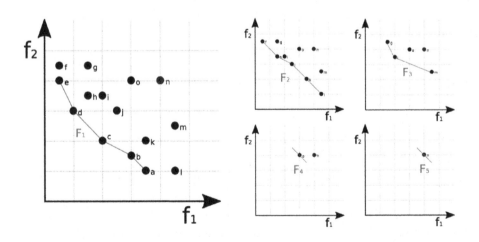

Figure 6.3. *Steps of the NDS algorithm for calculating successive fronts with two objectives functions to be optimized. The algorithm produces five fronts, F_1 to F_5*

The individuals in a Pareto front cannot be distinguished based solely on their objective values. For example, in Table 6.2, if we assume that the best individual is the one that minimizes the value of the objectives f_1 and f_2, we see that I_d is better than I_c on f_1, but that I_c is better than I_d on f_2.

The Pareto front gathers together *individuals that are not dominated by any other individuals in the population*. The conventional definition of dominance states that an *element x_1 dominates (is preferred to) an element $x_2(x_1 \dashv x_2)$ if x_1 is better than x_2 in at least one objective function and not worse with respect to all other objectives* [WEI 11, WEI 65].

If we apply this definition to the population $\{a..o\}$ shown in Figure 6.2, we find the following Pareto front of non-dominated individuals: $\{e, d, c, b, a\}$.

The NDS algorithm included in Goldberg and Deba's NSGA 2 calculates the successive fronts $F_{i..n}$ by re-evaluating and deleting non-dominated individuals $\{I_\varnothing\}$ within the population P at each step. For example, to calculate the next front F_2 in Figure 6.3, Deb proposes to delete all non-dominated individuals $I_\varnothing$ in the front F_1 of the population: $P_t = P_t - I_\varnothing$ before recalculating the new rank of the remaining individuals according to the dominance criterion. In this example, we delete the individuals $\{e, d, c, b, a\}$, and calculate the new Pareto front as $\{f, h, j, k, l\}$.

Individuals	$f1$	$f2$	Dominated by	Fitness value
a	3.5	1	$\varnothing$	1
b	3	1, 5	$\varnothing$	1
c	2	2	$\varnothing$	1
d	1	3	$\varnothing$	1
e	0.5	4	$\varnothing$	1
f	0.5	4.5	$\{e\}$	2
g	1.5	4.5	$\{d, e, f, h\}$	3
h	1.5	3.5	$\{d\}$	2
i	2	3.5	$\{c, d, h\}$	3
j	2.5	3	$\{c, d\}$	2
k	3.5	2	$\{a, b, c\}$	2
l	4.5	1	$\{a\}$	2
m	4.5	2.5	$\{a, b, c, k, l\}$	3
n	4	4	$\{a, b, c, d, e, h, i, j, k, o\}$	5
o	3	4	$\{b, c, d, e, h, i, j\}$	4

Table 6.2. *Example of fitness values calculated using the NDS algorithm with a population of individuals evaluated using two objective functions f_1, f_2*

6.3. Using NetLogo with OpenMOLE

6.3.1. *Presentation of OpenMOLE*

OpenMOLE allows us to construct, modify and execute workflows on distributed computing environments. A *workflow* may be viewed as a classical processing chain composed of various tasks/processing steps connected together with *transitions*. Unlike other existing workflow engines (Taverna, Kepler, etc.), OpenMOLE can integrate any kind of *task* into its workflow so long as it is available either in native form or as a software plugin (Figure 6.4). One such example is the NetLogo plugin, originally developed for Jéremy Fiegel's model, which we were able to reuse to seamlessly integrate the SimpopLocal model into our workflows. OpenMOLE can manage workflows with *complex topologies* involving loops, trigger conditions for transitions, aggregation, etc. One particular characteristic of OpenMOLE is the atomicity of tasks, which allows us to parallelize workflows without requiring the user to manage any of the drawbacks usually associated with competition.

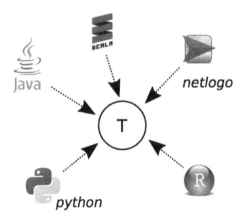

Figure 6.4. *Tasks can have different types*

The most significant difference from conventional processing chains is that the execution of any of these tasks may be *delegated* to *HPC environments* automatically and transparently, with (or without) an explicitly declared *experimental protocol*.

Each task has *inputs* and *outputs* that depend on processing. The workflows are executed in a similar manner to a fluid that is allowed to flow within a constrained environment, starting at a fixed point specified by the user, moving (or carried, in the spirit of the metaphor) from task to task by the transitions, which are responsible for the information submitted to them at the end of each processing step, until this fluid arrives at its destination. The values of the inputs become known at the point in time when the task is executed, based on the results that were produced and transmitted into the execution flow by previously executed tasks. After each processing step, the tasks can convey outputs to this flow, which will be transmitted to the next task.

Finally, workflows can be constructed by using a dedicated programming language (*Domain Specific Language* (DSL)[1]), or written interactively and graphically with a user interface. There is much more information on all of these concepts in publications on the software [REU 13], and its webpage. The best way to proceed is to give a very simple and visual example of a workflow that allows us to run a few replications of a NetLogo simulation model, as shown in Figure 6.5.

6.3.2. *Workflow for testing randomness*

The effect of randomness on model dynamics is difficult to pinpoint, but has a very strong impact on the results of exploration based on metaheuristics.

One of the ways to smooth the effects of randomness is to perform a certain number of *replications* when executing the simulations. This means repeatedly executing a simulation with identical parameter values but different random seeds with the goal of measuring the influence of randomness on variations in the measured objectives. It may come as a surprise that there is no "magic" number for the correct number of replications. It can depend on the measured objective, as well as on the values chosen for the parameters. More systematic exploration is required to begin to formulate an answer to this question. The shape of the distribution thus obtained is also unlikely to be Gaussian, which means that using the mean value to summarize the results is often not a good idea.

---

1 Dedicated languages provides a range of software-specific primitives to modelers for constructing and executing workflows, similar to how NetLogo handles Turtles.

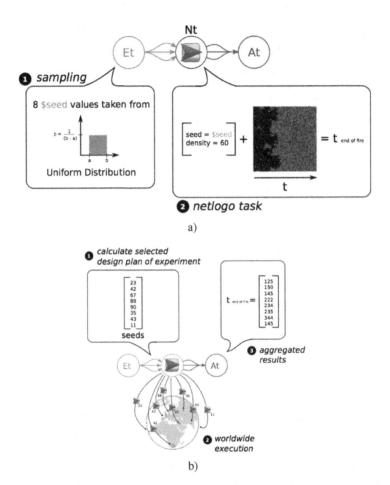

Figure 6.5. *a) When we first create a workflow, we need to parametrize the two first tasks, Et (Exploration task) and Nt (Netlogo task). For the exploration task Et, we have to choose a sampling that will allow us to generate the experimental protocol. The NetLogo model has to define its inputs and outputs: the $density$ parameter of the model is set to have value 60, but the **$seed** needs to be passed as an input to the task when it is executed in order for the model to work. The expected output of the model is the time t at which the fire definitively ends, and the model terminates: $t_{end-of-fire}$ b) The workflow is executed. The first step is to generate the experimental protocol. Values for the **$seed** are generated and assigned to future executions of the model (eight seeds for eight instances of the model). OpenMOLE manages the distribution of calculations, and the models are instantiated with the right parameters and executed in different parts of the world. Once all of the tasks have been executed, the 8 values of $t_{end-of-fire}$ are collected and aggregated in a list by the task At (Aggregation task)*

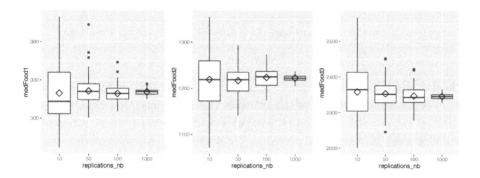

Figure 6.6. *Distribution of the median values of the three objective functions as a function of the number of replications with fixed parameter values. Each box shows the median value and quartiles, the lines show the maximum and minimum values, the dots are outliers and the diamonds are the mean values. The high dispersion of the values in the cases with fewer replications shows that if the number of replications is too low, any results obtained are unstable and might be due to chance*

To create this kind of chart, we perform 100 series of 10, 50, 100 and 1000 replications with a set of test parameter values set to $\{population = 125.0, diffusion - rate = 25.0, evaporation - rate = 25.0\}$. Other parameter values would likely yield different results.

In the example of *Ants*, we can clearly see that the value obtained for the objectives $medianFood1, medianFood2, medianFood3$ depends strongly on the number of replications. If the number of replications is too low, it is entirely possible that the optimizer will judge as satisfactory candidate solutions that only produce satisfactory fitness values "every now and again".

If performing the ideal/sufficient number of replications is not possible, which is often the case, it is a good idea to frequently re-evaluate the candidate solutions chosen by the optimizer. This is particularly important in the case of EAs based on a population of candidate solutions, as these algorithms retain and reuse the best individuals from each iteration. If an individual enters this population "by chance", it will continue to produce offspring whose estimated capacity is biased.

The workflow that allowed these results to be generated is composed of a chain of the following tasks (read from left to right), which we will go on to examine step-by-step.

```
exploration -< Strain(replication  -< (ants on env by 50) >- medians)
↪   hook saveHook
```

The first exploration task plans the exploration (symbolized by -<) of the series of replications, each of which involves executing a second exploration task named replication. The first exploration task will plan x_1 series of replications, each of which will contain x_2 replications of the ants model.

The ants task that defines the NetLogo model is executed by groups (50 simulations performed by each node) within the programming environment env (((ants on env by 50)) before aggregating the set of results (symbolized by >-), which allows the median to be calculated (one median for x_2 replications) by the medians task. The saveHook task is responsible for writing the results to a final csv file each time that a median is calculated.

The first exploration task of type ExplorationTask plans the execution of 100 series of replications (the variable i takes values from 0 to 100) with the following parameters for the Ants model (gPopulation = 125, gDiffusionRate = 25, gEvaporationRate = 25). These parameters are sent to the second exploration task *via* the outputs of this task.

```
val exploration = Capsule(
    ExplorationTask(i in (0.0 to 100.0 by 1.0)) set (
        name := "Series of replications",
        gPopulation := 125.0,
        gDiffusionRate:= 25.0,
        gEvaporationRate := 25.0,
        outputs += (gPopulation,gDiffusionRate,gEvaporationRate))
    )
```

When each exploration task is executed, it will call another ExplorationTask task named replication. This new task determines the number of model replications that are needed before aggregation.

```
val replication = Capsule(ExplorationTask(seed in
↪   (UniformDistribution[Int]() take 50)), strain = true)
```

In this task, we define 50 random seeds (seed variables) that will be transmitted with the other parameters that were already passed to the NetLogo task by the exploration task earlier in the workflow (via the option scala strain = true), which we describe below.

To define and use a NetLogo 5 model within an OpenMOLE workflow, we need to configure a Netlogo5Task, which we will then store in an ants variable.

This task takes two parameters, the system path pointing to a model file to load (./my/model/repository/ants.nlogo) and a list of NetLogo commands (see the cmds variable). Among the commands passed in this way, random ${ seed } sets a random seed value in NetLogo for the seed variable passed as an input to the task by OpenMOLE (substitution is indicated by ${ }), and run-to-grid is the function that begins the simulation.

The parameters that we want to vary (inputs) in the model, and the expected results from execution (outputs), are linked to variables declared in the OpenMOLE workflow by the methods netLogoInputs, netLogoOutputs, inputs, outputs. Thus, the gPopulation parameter is defined as a Val[Double] in the OpenMOLE workflow, and is linked to the global variable gpopulation in NetLogo by the command netLogoInputs += (gPopulation, *"gpopulation"*). This is equivalent to the set gpopulation value command, where value is given by the value of the variable gpopulation routed through the OpenMOLE workflow. Therefore, if an experimental protocol defined in OpenMOLE changes the value of gPopulation, this will be subsequently reflected in the simulation model.

```
// Define the input variables
val gPopulation = Val[Double]
val gDiffusionRate = Val[Double]
val gEvaporationRate = Val[Double]
val seed = Val[Int]

// Define the output variables
val food1 = Val[Double]
val food2 = Val[Double]
val food3 = Val[Double]
```

```
// Define the NetlogoTask
val cmds = Seq("random-seed ${seed}", "run-to-grid")

val ants =
  NetLogo5Task(workDirectory / "ants.nlogo", cmds) set (
    // Map the OpenMOLE variables to NetLogo variables
    netLogoInputs += (gPopulation, "gpopulation"),
    netLogoInputs += (gDiffusionRate, "gdiffusion-rate"),
    netLogoInputs += (gEvaporationRate, "gevaporation-rate"),
    netLogoOutputs += ("final-ticks-food1", food1),
    netLogoOutputs += ("final-ticks-food2", food2),
    netLogoOutputs += ("final-ticks-food3", food3),
    // The seed is used to control the initialization of the random
    ↪   number generator of NetLogo
    inputs += seed,
    outputs += seed
  )
```

OpenMOLE allows us to specify on which environment this NetLogo task ants will be executed. We could equally choose to use multiple processors on our local computer (val env = LocalEnvironment(5)) as cluster or grid computing (val env = EGIEnvironment("vo.complex-systems.eu")). The list of distributed environments compatible with OpenMOLE is described in more detail on the website of the software: http://www.openmole.org/

Once the 50 replications have been executed, OpenMOLE aggregates the results (>- operator) returned by the NetLogo task ants within the Scala task medians, which is responsible for calculating the medians of the results for each vector of 50 values associated with each objective function. Three new variables are required (medFood1, medFood2, medFood3) to store and transport the results of these calculations in the rest of the workflow as an output of the ants task.

```
val medFood1 = Val[Double]
val medFood2 = Val[Double]
val medFood3 = Val[Double]

val medians =
  Slot(ScalaTask("""
    import math.abs
```

```
val medFood1 = food1.median
val medFood2 = food2.median
val medFood3 = food3.median""") set (
name := "medians",
inputs += (food1.array, food2.array, food3.array),
outputs += (medFood1, medFood2, medFood3)
))
```

Finally, a hook ensures that the data are recovered and written into a csv file with each of the variables (gPopulation, gDiffusionRate, gEvaporationRate, medFood1, medFood2, medFood3) injected into the workflow by the various tasks.

```
val saveHook = AppendToCSVFileHook(workDirectory /
↪   "/results/replication/ants_100s_50r.csv", i, gPopulation,
↪   gDiffusionRate, gEvaporationRate, medFood1, medFood2, medFood3)
```

The syntax for describing workflows is liable to change, so the full and up-to-date workflow named ants_replication.oms is available on the GitHub repository for Chapter F in the folder scripts_experience/replications. Descriptions of the steps required to launch the four experiments (100 times 10, 50, 100 and 1000 replications) and generate the figures with R are given in the README file of this repository.

6.3.3. Workflow for calibrating with EA

The workflow for defining an optimization process that uses evolutionary algorithms is even simpler, since specialized tasks exist to encapsulate the complexity of these algorithms in OpenMOLE. To define and use these algorithm, OpenMOLE relies on a framework named MGO, which is available at the following link: https://github.com/openmole/mgo.

```
(evolution on env by 20 hook savePopulationHook)
```

The ants task is identical in every respect to the one described in the above workflow. The evolution task guides the exploration of the model based on metaheuristics.

The NGSA 2 algorithm that we described in this chapter is reproduced by this specialized NSGA2 task.

```
val nsga2 =
  NSGA2(
    mu = 200,
    genome = Seq(gPopulation in (25.0, 250.0), gDiffusionRate in (0.0,
    ↪   99.0), gEvaporationRate in (0.0, 99.0)),
    objectives = Seq(food1, food2, food3),
    replication = Replication(seed = seed, aggregation = Seq(median,
    ↪   median, median), max = 100)
  )
```

This task determines the following:

– the vector of genome values, i.e. the values that the optimizer is authorized to explore between the max and min bounds: gPopulation, : gDiffusionRate, : gEvaporationRate;

– the objective functions, already precalculated here as an output of the model: food1, : food2, : food3;

– the method for summarizing each vector of objectives, whose size is equivalent to the number of replications performed. In this example, the chosen method is to calculate the median of each objective. Within the framework of stochastic simulation, the optimizer relies on this vector of objective functions *in aggregate then summarized form* for evaluation.

How to manage the number of replications is left unspecified, allowing the optimizer to determine the most stable solutions that minimize this number during optimization, subject to a maximum of 100 authorized replications.

The task nsga2 is then passed as a parameter to an evolution task that specifies the type of execution when we execute this metaheuristic on a distributed computing environment.

```
val evolution =
  SteadyStateEvolution(
    algorithm = nsga2,
    evaluation = ants,
    parallelism = 500,
    termination = 2000
  )
```

There are several execution types, but here we chose a SteadyState distribution. Unlike conventional generation-based distributions, which wait until all candidate solutions have been evaluated before generating a new population of individuals for evaluation (offspring), this distribution generates new offspring "on the fly". Recall that, here, a candidate solution is a set of parameter values for the ants simulation, executed x times (where x is between 1 and 100). The median, calculated for each of the objectives over x replications, allows the optimizer to evaluate the quality of the candidate solution relative to other previously evaluated individuals present within the population. In other words, with this form of distribution, each previously evaluated candidate solution is directly compared to the rest of the general population based on the value of these objectives at time t before a new candidate solution is generated for evaluation (1 new offspring).

The parallelism parameter determines the number of simultaneous offspring, and therefore describes the degree of parallelism that we wish to introduce into the metaheuristic algorithm within the distributed environment. Without going into further detail, it is important to understand that this kind of evaluation allows the distributed calculation resources to be utilized much more efficiently and continuously than a generation-based distribution, in which these resources are only used in successive waves (we have to wait until each wave is complete before a new wave can be formed).

Finally, the termination parameter determines the stopping condition of the optimizer. This can be given in terms of a duration, but also a number of generations, as is the case here.

The OpenMOLE workflow named ants_calibration.oms corresponding to this experiment is available on the GitHub repository for Chapter F, in the folder scripts_experience/calibration. A description of the steps required to set this experiment up and generate a video showing how the optimization unfolds with the GnuPlot tool or R is also available in the README file of the same repository.

6.4. Analysis and interpretation of results

Calibration and model exploration generate a large body of data that is difficult to analyze directly. Optimizing an objective function with three parameters such as the one given above generates a table with the configuration of the Pareto front, which takes several hundreds of lines to specify the parameters (3 in this case) and objective values (3). Analyzing and interpreting the resulting file is a skill in its own right, but is necessary in order to understand how the simulation works.

6.4.1. *Analysis tools*

The data source to be analyzed is generally presented in the form of one or several CSV files generated by OpenMole (with one row per simulation and one column per parameter/variable). To analyze this kind of file, several tools are available, depending on user preferences and the type of analysis they wish to perform:

– *A spreadsheet (Excel, Calc, etc.)* can provide a quick initial overview. Pivot tables in Excel in particular can be used to calculate distributions with different filters. This solution has the advantage of being simple and quick, but does not support in-depth studies: the methods for statistical processing, graphical representation and processing large amounts of data are limited in current spreadsheet tools.

– The data can be explored with *NetLogo*. In Volume 1, we explained how to produce complex graphs with NetLogo (in particular scatter plots) and how to define one agent for each simulation point so that we can use the main view for visualization. By defining a user interface that allows us to select the axes (or generate the graphs in which we are interested), NetLogo lets us visualize datasets and even process them further. The advantage of this is that we do not have to define a new language for analysis, we preserve a certain degree of flexibility in interactions via the user interface, and similarly we can visualize the dynamics of the data. However, NetLogo is not specifically designed for data visualization, and performing statistical processing with some kinds of graphs (such as the box plot graph of Figure 6.6) can be difficult or impossible, whereas it would only take a few lines with a suitable analysis tool.

– Statistical processing software (such as **R**) allows us to easily process this kind of file and data. It requires us however to adapt to a new language. We will continue to use R (which we introduced in Volume 1), which has the advantage of being free and widely adopted within the scientific community, including the humanities.

6.4.2. *Choosing the graph*

Displaying data in the form of a graph helps us to both interpret and convey a message. Depending on the type of graph, the information that it contains will be very different: a distribution that is readily visible on a pie chart will be hidden on a curve. Given the range of types of graph that exist, it would be impossible to specify an exhaustive method for selecting which one to use. One potential first approach developed by Dr. Abela[2] is shown in Figure 6.7. This approach, which already differentiates between 21 possible cases, will however still need to be adapted to the application.

In our case, in which we analyze configurations of simulation agents, certain properties will guide the choice of which representation to use:

– *Particularly high numbers of variables*: the simple case of the Ant model already has 3 parameters and 3 objective variables. Graphs with 2 or 3 variables (in 3D) are generally insufficient to give an overview of the values of all variables. One possibility is to perform dimensionality reduction (e.g. with PCA). An alternative solution is to use a matrix of graphs such as that of Figure 6.8.

– *Inherent randomness of agent-based simulations*: Since agent-based simulations are stochastic models, each graph needs to show the results of multiple simulations. This is possible either by directly displaying multiple simulations (scatter plot), such as Figure 6.8, by displaying information relating to the distribution (diagonal of Figure 6.8), by showing the quartiles/deciles (box plot figures such as Figure 6.6), or finally by including information such as the standard deviation/variance.

---

2 http://extremepresentation.typepad.com/blog/2009/09/aide-%C3%A0-la-s%C3%A9lection-de-graphiques-chart-chooser-in-french.html.

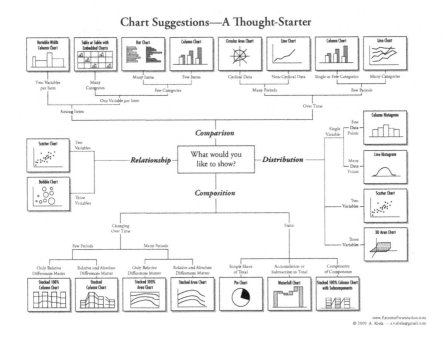

Figure 6.7. *Aide for choosing the chart type depending on the objective*

6.4.3. *Interpreting the results*

An evolutionary algorithm was used to find the minimum values for the objectives achieved by the *Ants* model. In other words, we ask the optimization algorithm to tell us, insofar as is possible, which parameter values (genome) would minimize the time (three objective functions $food1$, $food2$, $food3$) required to consume the heaps of food 1, 2 and 3. After a certain number of iterations, we obtain a population P comprised of the 200 best individuals obtained over 2000 generations (*population2000.csv*). The Pareto front (non-dominated individuals) is a subset of this population. Once the algorithm has converged satisfactorily to a relatively specific region of parameter values (see the video in the GitHub repository), we can consider this population as a whole without needing to recalculate the Pareto front. The corresponding results file generated by OpenMOLE is a CSV file consisting of 8 columns:

the 3 parameters (columns 2 to 4), the 3 variables describing the optimization (columns 5 to 7) and 2 variables describing the optimization (columns 1 and 8).

The solutions suggested by the algorithm can be described by 6 dimensions: the 3 dimensions corresponding to the parameters ($gPopulation, gDiffusionRate, gEvaporationRate$) and the 3 dimensions corresponding to the optimized variables ($food1, food2, food3$). Each of these dimensions is an important part of the solution description, which is why it is difficult to visualize the results of this algorithm. Matrices of graphs (*plot matrices*) like Figure 6.8 allow us to visualize all pairs of variables (pivot charts or scatter plots), and give information relating to the variables on the diagonal (single distribution). The advantage of R is that these kinds of graphs can be generated in 2 lines: one to load the data, and another to display the graph (listing 6.4).

```
library(httr)
library(GGally)
library(readr)
4
calibration<-read_csv("./calibration/resultats/population2000.csv")
ggpairs(data=calibration,
  columns=c(2:7),
  upper = list(continuous = wrap("density", alpha = 0.5)),
9  lower = list(continuous = "points"),
  diag = list(continuous = "barDiag"),
  title="scatter matrix")
```

Listing 6.4. *R code to read data and generate a matrix of graphs (like in Figure 6.8 without the clusters)*

The code in listing 6.4 (which requires libraries for graphics and importing, which are loaded at the start) allows us to: 1) import the data obtained at the end of optimization; 2) create a matrix of graphs by specifying which CSV columns should be used (columns 2 to 7), the type of graph to show on the diagonal ($diag$ =), above the diagonal ($upper$ =), and below the diagonal ($lower$ =). In our case, we chose to display the densities as a histogram on the diagonal, to show points (scatter plots) below the diagonal, and densities (contours) above. This type of graph (which is exactly equivalent to Figure 6.8 except without different types of points) already provides us with a global description of the results.

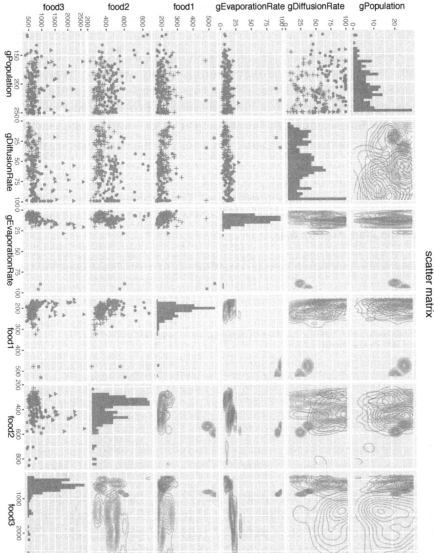

Figure 6.8. *Matrix of graphs describing pairs of variables for 200 configurations obtained after 2000 optimization steps. The graphs on the diagonal of the matrices describe the distribution of the values of each variable. The graphs under the diagonal represent the values of each configuration of pairs of variables with one point per configuration (scatter plot). The graphs above the diagonal show the same information in the form of densities (contours). The configurations are organized into 4 groups obtained by clustering and identified by color/shape. For a color version of the figure, see www.iste.co.uk/banos/netlogo2.zip*

The diagonal of the graph allows us to describe each of the variables individually. We can see that almost all configurations have low evaporation rates and rather high populations. The diffusion rate on the other hand is distributed homogeneously, peaking at the maximum value (100). The distributions of the objective variables also vary: $food1$ takes low values (less than 300 except for 2 around 500), $food2$ has a relatively wide distribution of up to 600 and $food3$ has a dense distribution up to 1000 and a tail up to 2500. The absolute values of the objective functions are important here, more so than for the values of the parameters, since they are directly comparable (they represent the number of steps before the food is exhausted). Food source 1 always runs out quickly: even for the two other cases that seem high, their value (500) is located around the average of source 2, which would be comparatively low for source 3.

In order to more accurately describe the configurations thus obtained, it is helpful to reorder them into groups. This makes it easier to acquire a global overview of the properties of a given set of configurations. Although it is relatively easy to describe the group of 2 configurations with high $food1$ values (the two points are relatively distinct from the others), it is not so easy to locate the other groups of configurations on the graph. To gather these configurations together, we can group the points using a clustering algorithm. We must bear in mind that this analysis is done with a stable population of evaluated solutions, and therefore revolves very tightly around a few key types of behavior exhibited by the boundaries, which inform the modeler about the contradictions that the optimization algorithm must face to minimize these three objectives simultaneously. We can clearly see that the gaps vary strongly depending on the objectives, which can sometimes create problems for the optimizer.

In our case, we will use a simple clustering algorithm (KMeans with 4 classes) with the 6 dimensions of the parameters and the variables, and after normalizing the values (so that they are homogeneous across different scales). Clustering then allows us to identify configurations by comparing different matrix cells using color coding and shapes (Figure 6.8). The full code of the graph, including clustering, is given in listing 6.5.

```
  install.packages("httr")
  install.packages("plotly")
  install.packages("GGally")
4 install.packages("readr")
  install.packages("factoextra")

  library(httr)
  library(plotly)
9 library(GGally)
  library(readr)
  library(factoextra)

  calibration<-read_csv("./calibration/resultats/population2000.csv")
14
  calibration_clust<-calibration[2:7]
  calibration_clust<-scale(calibration_clust)
  km.res <- kmeans(calibration_clust, 4, nstart = 25)
  calibration$clust=as.factor(km.res$cluster)
19
  pp=ggpairs(data=calibration,
             columns=c(2:7),
             upper = list(continuous = wrap("density", alpha = 0.5)),
             lower = list(continuous = "points"),
24           diag = list(continuous = "barDiag"),
             title="scatter matrix",
             mapping=aes(color=clust,shape=clust))
  print(pp)
```

Listing 6.5. *Full R script for generating a matrix of graphs using clustering to divide up and regroup the points (results in Figure 6.8)*

Using these groups and all of cells of the matrix, we can describe the configurations obtained by the EA more precisely:

– The first configuration (blue square) corresponds to the two solutions with high $food1$ values identified earlier. This configuration is interesting because it is the only one with a high value for the evaporation rate. It shows the benefit of exploring with EAs, as they succeed in finding this kind of configuration, which despite being very different from the others is nonetheless effective: by combining a high evaporation rate with a high population and low diffusion, we can achieve good results for two of the three objectives ($food2$ and $food3$), and slightly worse results for $food1$.

– Distinguishing between the three other configurations is easy on the scatter plot and contour plot of the pair $food3/gDiffusionRate$:

configuration 2 (purple cross) has a low diffusion rate, configuration 3 (red circle) has a high diffusion rate and configuration 4 (green triangle) has high values for $food3$:

- if we examine configuration 2 (purple cross), we can see on the distribution graphs that it is characterized by low rates of evaporation and diffusion. Combining these two (which is made possible by a high population) leads to especially good results for the $food2$ indicator (and reasonable results for $food1$ and $food3$);

- the third configuration (red circle) has high diffusion. This situation (which is compatible with but does not require low population) leads to good results for $food1$ and average results for $food2$ and $food3$;

- finally, configuration 4 (green triangle) is the one with low (or even very low) success in terms of $food3$ (high values). This configuration can be described as an extreme version of configuration 3: with a smaller population, even higher diffusion rates and evaporation rates that are also higher, we achieve poor results on $food3$ but we still get good results for $food1$ and $food2$.

6.5. Conclusion

The integrated exploration tools in NetLogo quickly reach their limits as models become larger and require greater numbers of parameters: only exhaustive exploration of the parameter space is available for the *behavior space* and the available metaheuristics are limited (they do not support multiple objectives); parallelization is limited to only the cores available on the computer on which NetLogo is running; the choice of graphs offered by NetLogo is limited.

Using external tools such as R and OpenMOLE has proven to be invaluable. R allows us to analyze simulation results with a vast panel of statistical tools. OpenMOLE supports access to distributed computing power (grid computing, *clusters*) that can significantly reduce the computation time from several days or even years to a few minutes or hours.

Exploration tools such as OpenMOLE have become essential today, and will continue to gain in popularity in future. These platforms will gradually move closer to end users by incorporating general-purpose toolkits and other more specialized toolkits for specific applications, with increasingly simple and user-friendly syntax for describing models.

Conclusion

Agent-based models can help us to understand and explore spatial systems! Agent-based modeling is flexible, intuitive and is closely connected to both data and theory, which gives it a very special role within most scientific communities. These models are as much tools for understanding, exploring and writing scenarios as they are a medium for cross-disciplinary exchange. Following on from Volume 1, *Agent-based Spatial Modeling with NetLogo* [BAN 15a], which discusses how to model spatial phenomena with agents from a methodological and practical perspective, this second volume has attempted to be both more advanced and more open. It uses examples to show that very sophisticated models can be developed and operated in NetLogo, in particular due to the possibilities of dynamic coupling with specialized extensions and other libraries, software programs and platforms. In this spirit, a range of fundamental topics have been selected for discussion and systematically illustrated with examples: multi-scale modeling, coupling of micro/macro models based on networks, analysis of dynamic graphs, swarm problem-solving, as well as the implementation of complex model exploration protocols, all of which represent thriving areas of research that can be explored with NetLogo in a way that could almost be described as "experimental".

Chapter written by Arnaud BANOS, Christophe LANG and Nicolas MARILLEAU.

Bibliography

[ABO 14] ABOUAÏSSA H., KUBERA Y., MORVAN G., "Dynamic hybrid traffic flow modeling", *arXiv preprint, arXiv:1401.6773*, 2014.

[ADE 13] ADE P., AGHANIM N., ARMITAGE-CAPLAN C. *et al.*, "Planck 2013 results. I. Overview of products and scientific results", *arXiv preprint, arXiv:1303.5062*, 2013.

[ADL 94] ADLEMAN L.M., "Molecular computation of solutions to combinatorial problems", *Science*, vol. 266, no. 5187, pp. 1021–1024, November 1994.

[ADL 98] ADLEMAN L.M., "Computing with DNA", *Scientific American*, vol. 279, no. 8, pp. 34–41, 1998.

[AMB 06] AMBLARD F., ROUCHIER J., BOMMEL P., "Evaluation et validation de modèles multi-agents", in AMBLARD F., PHAN D. (eds), *Modélisation et Simulation Multi-Agents*, Hermes Science-Lavoisier, pp. 103–120, 2006.

[AWA 13] AWAIS M.U., MUELLER W., ELSHEIKH A. *et al.*, "Using the HLA for distributed continuous simulations", in *2013 8th EUROSIM Congress on Modeling and Simulation*, IEEE, pp. 544–549, 2013.

[AXE 97] AXELROD R., "The dissemination of culture: a model with local convergence and global polarization", *Journal of Conflict Resolution*, vol. 41, no. 2, pp. 203–226, 1997.

[BAK 93] BAKIS H., *Les Réseaux et leurs enjeux sociaux*, Presses universitaires de France, Paris, 1993.

[BAN 09] BANOS A., "Simulating pedestrian behavior in complex and dynamic environments: An agent-based perspective", in BAVAUD F., MAGER C. (eds), *European Handbook of Theoretical and Quantitative Geography*, FGSE, Lausanne, pp. 1–27, 2009.

[BAN 15a] BANOS A., LANG C., MARILLEAU N. (eds), *Agent-based Spatial Simulation with NetLogo 1*, ISTE Press Ltd, London and Elsevier Ltd, Oxford, 2015.

[BAN 15b] BANOS A., CORSON N., GAUDOU B. *et al.*, "The importance of being hybrid for spatial epidemic models: a multi-scale approach", *Systems*, vol. 3, no. 4, pp. 309–329, 2015.

[BAN 16] BANOS A., CORSON N., GAUDOU B. *et al.*, "Coupling micro and macro dynamics models on networks: application to disease spread", in *Multi-Agent Based Simulation XVI, International Workshop, MABS 2015*, Istanbul, Turkey, pp. 19–33, 2016.

[BAR 99] BARABÁSI A.-L., ALBERT R., "Emergence of scaling in random networks", *Science*, vol. 286, no. 5439, pp. 509–512, 1999.

[BEL 61] BELLMAN R.E., *Adaptive Control Processes: A Guided Tour*, MIT Press, 1961.

[BEN 93] BENI G., WANG J., "Swarm intelligence in cellular robotic systems", in DARIO P., SANDINI G., AEBISCHER P. (eds), *Robots and Biological Systems: Towards a New Bionics?*, Springer Berlin Heidelberg, 1993.

[BER 81] BERTHO-LAVENIR C., CARRÉ P.-A., GUERRIER C., *Télégraphes et Téléphones: de Valmy au Microprocesseur*, Librairie générale française, Paris, 1981.

[BER 90] BERRY G., BOUDOL G., "The chemical abstract machine", in *Proceedings of the 17th ACM SIGPLAN-SIGACT Symposium on Principles of Programming Languages*, New York, pp. 81–94, 1990.

[BER 06] BERTELLE C., DUTOT A., GUINAND F. *et al.*, "Organization detection using emergent computing", *International Transactions on Systems Science and Applications*, vol. 2, no. 1, pp. 61–69, 2006.

[BER 10] BERGEZ J., GARCIA F., RAYNAL H., "RECORD: an integrated framework to build, evaluate and simulate cropping systems", in *Agro2010'the XIth ESA Congress*, Agropolis International Editions, Montpellier, pp. 929–930, 2010.

[BIA 12] BIADA L., "Ant cemetery", https://flickr.com/photos/pedroscreamerovsky/69115494 46, April 2012.

[BLA 09] BLANCHART E., MARILLEAU N., CHOTTE J.-L. *et al.*, "SWORM: an agent-based model to simulate the effect of earthworms on soil structure", *European Journal of Soil Science*, vol. 60, no. 1, pp. 13–21, 2009.

[BON 76] BONDY J.A., MURTY U.S.R., *Graph Theory with Applications*, Macmillan, 1976.

[BON 97a] BONABEAU E., THERAULAZ G., "Auto-organisation et comportements collectifs: La modélisation des sociétés d'insectes", in THERAULAZ G., SPITZ F. (eds), *Auto-Organisation et Comportement*, Hermes Science, Paris, pp. 91–140, 1997.

[BON 97b] BONABEAU E., THERAULAZ G., DENEUBOURG J.-L. *et al.*, "Self-organization in social insects", *Trends in Ecology & Evolution*, vol. 12, no. 5, pp. 188–193, 1997.

[BON 99] BONABEAU E., DORIGO M., THERAULAZ G., *Swarm Intelligence, From Natural to Artificial Swarm Intelligence*, Oxford University Press, 1999.

[BOU 01] BOUZY B., CAZENAVE T., "Computer go: an AI oriented survey", *Artificial Intelligence*, vol. 132, no. 33, pp. 39–103, 2001.

[BOU 03] BOURREL E., Modélisation dynamique de l'écoulement du trafic routier: du macroscopique au microscopique, PhD thesis, University Nice Sophia Antipolis, 2003.

[BRA 01] BRANDES U., "A faster algorithm for betweenness centrality", *Journal of Mathematical Sociology*, vol. 25, no. 2, pp. 163–177, 2001.

[BUL 05] BULLE N., "Les modèles formels et l'explication en sciences sociales", *L'Année Sociologique*, vol. 55, no. 1, p. 19, 2005.

[BUR 06] BURGHOUT W., KOUTSOPOULOS H., "Hybrid traffic simulation models: vehicle loading at meso–micro boundaries", in *International Symposium of Transport Simulation*, 2006.

[CLE 02] CLERC M., KENNEDY J., "The particle swarm – explosion, stability, and convergence in a multidimensional complex space", *IEEE Transactions on Evolutionary Computation*, IEEE, vol. 6, no. 1, pp. 58–73, 2002.

[COL 91] COLORNI A., DORIGO M., MANIEZZO V., "Distributed optimization by ant colonies", in *Proceedings of the First European Conference on Artificial Life*, Paris, pp. 134–142, vol. 142, 1991.

[CRE 95] CRESPI B.J., YANEGA D., "The definition of eusociality", *Behavioral Ecology*, vol. 6, no. 1, pp. 109–115, 1995.

[DAU 14] DAUDÉ E., LAPERRIÈRE V., LEMOY R. *et al.*, "EpiSim: simulation d'épidémies", in MAPS C. (ed.), *Recueil de Fiches Pédagogiques du Réseau MAPS*, pp. 47–68, July 2014.

[DEB 00] DEB K., AGRAWAL S., PRATAP A. *et al.*, "A fast elitist non-dominated sorting genetic algorithm for multi-objective optimization: NSGA-II", *Lecture Notes in Computer Science*, vol. 1917, pp. 849–858, 2000.

[DEN 90] DENEUBOURG J.-L., ARON S., GOSS S. *et al.*, "The self-organizing exploratory pattern of the Argentine ant", *Journal of Insect Behavior*, vol. 3, no. 2, pp. 159–168, March 1990.

[DEN 91] DENEUBOURG J.-L., GOSS S., FRANKS N. *et al.*, "The dynamics of collective sorting robot-like ants and ant-like robots", *Proceedings of the First International Conference on Simulation of Adaptive Behavior on From Animals to Animats*, pp. 356–363, 1991.

[DIJ 71] DIJKSTRA E.W., *A Short Introduction to the Art of Programming*, Technische Hogeschool, vol. 4, 1971.

[EBE 95] EBERHART R., KENNEDY J., "A new optimizer using particle swarm theory", in *Proceedings of the Sixth International Symposium on Micro Machine and Human Science*, New York, vol. 1, pp. 39–43, 1995.

[ERD 59] ERDŐS P., RÉNYI A., "On random graphs", *Publicationes Mathematicae Debrecen*, vol. 6, pp. 290–297, 1959.

[EUL 41] EULER L., "Solutio problemata ad geometriam situs pertinentis, Commentarii Academiae Scientiarum Imperialis Petropolitanae", *Commentarii Academiae Scientiarum Petropolitanae*, vol. 8, pp. 128–140, available at https://math.dartmouth.edu/ēuler/docs/originals/E053.pdf, 1741.

[FER 97] FERBER J., PERROT J.-F., *Les Systèmes Multi-Agents: Vers une Intelligence Collective*, InterEditions, Paris, 1997.

[FOR 91] FORREST S., *Emergent Computation*, MIT Press, 1991.

[FOR 10] FORTUNATO S., "Community detection in graphs", *Physics Reports*, vol. 486, nos. 3–5, pp. 75–174, 2010.

[FOR 11] FORD L.R., FULKERSON D.R., *Flows in Networks*, Princeton University Press, 2011.

[GAU 07] GAUBERT L., REDOU P., HARROUET F. *et al.*, "Analyse mathématique du tri du couvain par les fourmis: auto-organisation fonctionnelle dénuée d'intelligence collective", in CAMPS V., MATHIEU P. (eds), *JFSMA 2007*, Cepadues Editions, pp. 13–22, 2007.

[GIB 15] GIBSON M.J., KEEDWELL E.C., SAVI D.A., "An investigation of the efficient implementation of cellular automata on multi-core CPU and GPU hardware", *Journal of Parallel and Distributed Computing*, vol. 77, pp. 11–25, 2015.

[GIL 59] GILBERT E.N., "Random graphs", *The Annals of Mathematical Statistics*, vol. 30, no. 4, pp. 1141–1144, 1959.

[GIR 02] GIRVAN M., NEWMAN M.E.J., "Community structure in social and biological networks", *Proceedings of the National Academy of Sciences*, vol. 99, no. 12, pp. 7821–7826, 2002.

[GOD 07] GODARA A., LASSARRE S., BANOS A., "Simulating pedestrian-vehicle interaction in an urban network using cellular automata and multi-agent models", in SCHADSCHNEIDER A., PÖSCHEL T., KÜHNE R. *et al.* (eds), *Traffic and Granular Flow '05*, Springer, pp. 411–418, 2007.

[GOL 89] GOLDBERG D.E., *Genetic Algorithms in Search, Optimization, and Machine Learning*, Addison-Wesley, 1989.

[GOS 89] GOSS S., ARON S., DENEUBOURG J.L. *et al.*, "Self-organized shortcuts in the Argentine ant", *Naturwissenschaften*, vol. 76, no. 12, pp. 579–581, 1989.

[GRA 59] GRASSÉ P.-P., "La reconstruction du nid et les coordinations interindividuelles chez *Bellicositermes Natalensis* et *Cubitermes sp.* la théorie de la stigmergie: Essai d'interprétation du comportement des termites constructeurs", *Insectes Sociaux*, vol. 6, no. 1, pp. 41–80, March 1959.

[GRE 35] GREENSHIELDS B., CHANNING W., MILLER H. *et al.*, "A study of traffic capacity", in *Highway Research Board Proceedings*, National Research Council (USA), 1935.

[GRI 05] GRIMM V., REVILLA E., BERGER U. *et al.*, "Pattern-oriented modeling of agent-based complex systems: lessons from ecology", *Science* vol. 310, no. 5750, pp. 987–991, November 2005.

[HAM 10] HAMDI A., ANTOINE V., MONMARCHÉ N. *et al.*, "Artificial ants for automatic classification", in MONMARCHÉ N., GUINAND F., SIARRY P. (eds), *Artificial Ants. From Collective Intelligence to Real-life Optimization and Beyond*, Wiley, pp. 266–287, 2010.

[HAR 28] HARVEY W., LEAKE C.D., *Exercitatio Anatomica de Motu Cordis et Sanguinis in Animalibus*, available at http://www.biodiversitylibrary.org/bibliography/6405, Springfield III: Thomas, 1928.

[HAS 12] HASSOUMI I., LANG C., MARILLEAU N. *et al.*, "Toward a spatially-centered approach to integrate heterogeneous and multi-scales urban component models", in *Advances on Practical Applications of Agents and Multi-Agent Systems – 10th International Conference on Practical Applications of Agents and Multi-Agent Systems*, pp. 81–86, 2012.

[HEP 90] HEPPNER F., GRENANDER U., "A stochastic nonlinear model for coordinated bird flocks", in KRASSNER S., (eds.), *The Ubiquity of Chaos*, AAAS, pp. 233–238, 1990.

[HEW 73] HEWITT C., BISHOP P., STEIGER R., "A universal modular ACTOR formalism for artificial intelligence", in *Proceedings of the 3rd International Joint Conference on Artificial Intelligence*, San Francisco, pp. 235–245, 1973.

[HOL 92] HOLLAND J.H., *Adaptation in Natural and Artificial Systems*, MIT Press, 1992.

[KEN 01] KENNEDY J., EBERHART R.C., *Swarm Intelligence*, Morgan Kaufmann Publishers, 2001.

[KER 27] KERMACK W.O., MCKENDRICK A.G., "A contribution to the mathematical theory of epidemics", *Proceedings of the Royal Society of London A: Mathematical, Physical and Engineering Sciences*, vol. 115, no. 772, pp. 700–721, 1927.

[KIR 83] KIRKPATRICK S., GELATT C.D., VECCHI M.P., "Optimization by simulated annealing", *Science*, vol. 220, no. 4598, pp. 671–680, 1983.

[KUB 11] KUBERA Y., MATHIEU P., PICAULT S., "IODA: an interaction-oriented approach for multi-agent based simulations", *Autonomous Agents and Multi-Agent Systems*, vol. 23, no. 3, pp. 303–343, 2011.

[KÖN 90] KÖNIG D., *Theory of Finite and Infinite Graphs*, Birkhäuser, Boston, 1990.

[LAP 92] LAPORTE G., "The traveling salesman problem: An overview of exact and approximate algorithms", *European Journal of Operational Research*, vol. 59, no. 2, pp. 231–247, 1992.

[LEB 96] LEBACQUE J.-P., "The Godunov scheme and what it means for first order traffic flow models", *Internaional Symposium on Transportation and Traffic Theory*, pp. 647–677, 1996.

[LEM 90] LEMOIGNE J.-L., "La mémoire du réseau: tout s'écoule... et pourtant", *Flux*, vol. 6, no. 2, pp. 25–32, 1990.

[LIG 55] LIGHTHILL M.J., WHITHAM G.B., "On kinematic waves. II. A theory of traffic flow on long crowded roads", *Proceedings of the Royal Society of London A: Mathematical, Physical and Engineering Sciences*, vol. 229, no. 1178, pp. 317–345, 1955.

[MAR 02] MARTIN M., CHOPARD B., ALBUQUERQUE P., "Formation of an ant cemetery: swarm intelligence or statistical accident?", *Future Generation Computer Systems*, vol. 18, no. 7, pp. 951–959, 2002.

[MCC 04] MCCONNELL S., *Code Complete, Second Edition*, Microsoft Press, 2004.

[MIC 69] MICHENER C.D., "Comparative social behavior of bees", *Annual Review of Entomology*, vol. 14, no. 1, pp. 299–342, 1969.

[MOR 77] MORIN E., *La méthode, Tome 1: la nature de la nature*, Seuil, Paris, 1977.

[MUS 03] MUSSO P., *Critique des réseaux*, Presses universitaires de France, 2003.

[NAG 92] NAGEL K., SCHRECKENBERG M., "A cellular automaton model for freeway traffic", *Journal de Physique I*, vol. 2, no. 12, pp. 2221–2229, 1992.

[NAT 09] ÉDUCATION NATIONALE, "Épreuve de Mathématiques – Spécialité du baccalauréat ES", 2009.

[NEW 04] NEWMAN M.E., GIRVAN M., "Finding and evaluating community structure in networks", *Physical Review E*, vol. 69, no. 2, p. 026113, 2004.

[NEW 06] NEWMAN M.E., "Modularity and community structure in networks", *Proceedings of the National Academy of Sciences*, vol. 103, no. 23, pp. 8577–8582, 2006.

[QUE 05] QUESNEL G., DUBOZ R., VERSMISSE D. *et al.*, "DEVS coupling of spatial and ordinary differential equations: VLE framework", *OICIMS*, vol. 5, pp. 281–294, 2005.

[RAG 07] RAGHAVAN U.N., ALBERT R., KUMARA S., "Near linear time algorithm to detect community structures in large-scale networks", *Physical Review E*, vol. 76, no. 3, p. 036106, 2007.

[REG 11] REGO C., GAMBOA D., GLOVER F. *et al.*, "Traveling salesman problem heuristics: Leading methods, implementations and latest advances", *European Journal of Operational Research*, vol. 211, no. 3, pp. 427–441, June 2011.

[RES 94] RESNICK M., *Turtles, Termites, and Traffic Jams*, MIT Press, 1994.

[REU 13] REUILLON R., LECLAIRE M., REY-COYREHOURCQ S., "OpenMOLE, a workflow engine specifically tailored for the distributed exploration of simulation models", *Future Generation Computer Systems*, vol. 29, no. 8, pp. 1981–1990, 2013.

[REY 87] REYNOLDS C.W., "Flocks, herds and schools: A distributed behavioral model", *Computer Graphics*, vol. 21, no. 4, pp. 25–34, 1987.

[REY 15] REY-COYREHOURCQ S., "Une plateforme intégrée pour la construction et l'évaluation de modèles de simulation en géographie", available at http://these.sebastienreycoyrehourcq.fr/, 2015.

[RIC 56] RICHARDS P. I., "Shock waves on the highway", *Operations Research*, vol. 4, no. 1, pp. 42–51, 1956.

[ROU 16] ROUSSET A., HERRMANN B., LANG C. *et al.*, "Using nested graphs to distribute parallel and distributed multi-agent systems", *in International Conference on Parallel, Distributed, and Network-Based Processing*, 2016.

[SAU 93] SAUSSURE F.D., BALLY C., DE MAURO T., *Cours de Linguistique Générale*, Payot, 1993.

[SCH 95] SCHRECKENBERG M., SCHADSCHNEIDER A., NAGEL K. *et al.*, "Discrete stochastic models for traffic flow", *Physical Review E*, vol. 51, no. 4, p. 2939, 1995.

[SCH 02] SCHADSCHNEIDER A., "Traffic flow: a statistical physics point of view", *Physica A: Statistical Mechanics and its Applications*, vol. 313, no. 1, pp. 153–187, 2002.

[SCH 15] SCHMITT C., REY-COYREHOURCQ S., REUILLON R. *et al.*, "Half a billion simulations: Evolutionary algorithms and distributed computing for calibrating the simpoplocal geographical model", *Environment and Planning B: Planning and Design*, vol. 42, no. 2, pp. 300–315, 2015.

[SCU 01] SCULTETUS A.H., VILLAVICENCIO J., RICH N.M., "Facts and fiction surrounding the discovery of the venous valves", *Journal of Vascular Surgery*, vol. 33, no. 2, pp. 435–441, 2001.

[THE 02] THERAULAZ G., BONABEAU E., NICOLIS S.C. *et al.*, "Spatial patterns in ant colonies", *Proceedings of the National Academy of Sciences*, vol. 99, no. 15, pp. 9645–9649, 2002.

[THI 10] THIELE J.C., GRIMM V., "NetLogo meets R: Linking agent-based models with a toolbox for their analysis", *Environmental Modelling and Software*, vol. 25, no. 8, pp. 972–974, 2010.

[TRE 08] TREUIL J.-P., DROGOUL A., ZUCKER J.-D., *Modélisation et Simulation à Base d'Agents*, Dunod, 2008.

[TRO 07] TROMP J., FARNEBACK G., "Combinatorics of Go", in VAN DEN HERIK, CIANCARINI H., DONKERS P. (eds.), *Computers and Games*, pp. 72–83, Springer, 2007.

[TUT 63] TUTTE W.T., "How to draw a graph", *Proceedings of the London Mathematical Society*, vol. 3-13, no. 1, pp. 743–767, 1963.

[UND 61] UNDERWOOD R.T., "Speed, volume, and density relationships", Bureau of Highway Traffic, Yale University, 1961.

[VAL 12] VALCKE S., BALAJI V., CRAIG A. *et al.*, "Coupling technologies for earth system modelling", *Geoscientific Model Development*, vol. 5, no. 6, pp. 1589–1596, 2012.

[VON 66] VON NEUMANN J.V., *Theory of Self-Reproducing Automata*, University of Illinois Press, 1966.

[WAG 15] VAN WAGENINGEN-KESSELS F., VAN LINT H., VUIK K. *et al.*, "Genealogy of traffic flow models", *EURO Journal on Transportation and Logistics*, vol. 4, no. 4, pp. 445–473, 2015.

[WAT 98] WATTS D.J., STROGATZ S.H., "Collective dynamics of 'small-world' networks", *Nature*, vol. 393, no. 6684, pp. 440–442, 1998.

[WEI 99] WEISS G. (ed.), *Multiagent Systems: A Modern Approach to Distributed Artificial Intelligence*, MIT Press, 1999.

[WEI 11] WEISE T., Global Optimization Algorithms – Theory and Application, available at: www.it-weise.de, 2011.

[WIL 97] WILENSKY U.J., "NetLogo Ants model", Center for Connected Learning and Computer-based Modeling, Northwestern University, available at http://ccl.northwestern. edu/netlogo/models/Ants, 1997.

[WIL 00] WILSON E.O., *Sociobiology: the New Synthesis*, Belknap Press of Harvard University Press, 2000.

[WIL 05] WILSON E.O., HOLLDOBLER B., "Eusociality: Origin and consequences", *Proceedings of the National Academy of Sciences*, vol. 102, no. 38, pp. 13367–13371, 2005.

[WIL 13] WILENSKY U., "Mouse Drag One Example", https://modelingcommons.org/ browse/one_model/2330#model_tabs_browse_info, 2013.

[ZEI 97] ZEIGLER B.P., MOON Y., KIM D. *et al.*, "The DEVS environment for high-performance modeling and simulation", *IEEE Computational Science & Engineering*, vol. 4, no. 3, pp. 61–71, 1997.

List of Authors

Stefan BALEV
LITIS – NORMASTIC FR
CNRS 3638
University of Le Havre
France

Arnaud BANOS
UMR Géographie-cités
CNRS, University of Paris 1
Panthéon-Sorbonne
University of Paris 7 Diderot
France

Philippe CAILLOU
LRI Laboratory
University of Paris Sud
Orsay
France

Nathalie CORSON
University of Normandy
UNIHAVRE, LMAH
FR-CNRS-3335
ISCN
Le Havre
France

Éric DAUDE
UMR IDEES 6266
CNRS
Rouen
France

Antoine DUTOT
LITIS – NORMASTIC FR
CNRS 3638
University of Le Havre
France

Benoit GAUDOU
IRIT Laboratory
University Toulouse 1 Capitole
Toulouse
France

Christophe LANG
Institut FEMTO-ST/DISC
UMR 6174, CNRS
University of Burgundy
Franche-Comté
Besançon
France

Nicolas MARILLEAU
UMI 209 UMMISCO
IRD-UPMC
Bondy
France

Jean-Marc NICOD
Institut FEMTO-ST/AS2M
UMR 6174, ENSMM, CNRS
University of Burgundy
Franche-Comté
Besançon
France

Damien OLIVIER
LITIS – NORMASTIC FR
CNRS 3638
University of Le Havre
France

Sébastien REY COYREHOURCQ
UMR IDEES 6266
CNRS
Rouen
France

Guilhelm SAVIN
LITIS – NORMASTIC FR
CNRS 3638
University of Le Havre
France

Patrick TAILLANDIER
MIAT, INRA
Toulouse
France

Index

Printed in the United States
By Bookmasters